Test Prep and Admissions

The Ring of McAllister

A Score-Raising Mystery Featuring
1,046 Must-Know Vocabulary Words
for the New SAT

by Robert Marantz

Simon & Schuster

NEW YORK · LONDON · SYDNEY · TORONTO

Kaplan Publishing
Published by Simon & Schuster
1230 Avenue of the Americas
New York, NY 10020

For bulk sales to schools, colleges, and universities, please contact: Order
Department, Simon and Schuster, 100 Front Street, Riverside, NJ 08075.
Phone: (800) 223-2336. Fax: (800) 943-9831.

Editor: Ruth Baygell
Cover Design: Cheung Tai
Interior Page Layout: Renée Mitchell
Production Manager: Michael Shevlin
Executive Editor: Jennifer Farthing

Manufactured in the United States of America
Published simultaneously in Canada

November 2004

10 9 8 7 6 5 4 3 2 1

ISBN: 0-7432-6577-7

TABLE OF CONTENTS

Acknowledgments

This book is dedicated to two Bens:

My nephew, for reminding me that the world is a magnificent place filled with new discoveries; and my father, for being my most ardent fan and instilling in me the motivation to be my best.

Thanks also go to my family—Carole, Bruce, and Darlene Marantz—for always encouraging me in my creative endeavors; Ruth Baygell at Kaplan Books for her editorial acumen; Maureen McMahon at Simon & Schuster; and Del Franz at Kaplan Books.

Finally, this book could not have been written without the love, support, insight, intelligence, and countless contributions of one very special person. Preeti, you are my beacon, my paragon, my everything. Thank you.

About the Author

A graduate of Cornell University, Robert Marantz was a project manager for Kaplan, Inc., during which time he co-wrote the best-selling Higher Score series of test preparation software. He has also authored several screenplays and television scripts. He currently makes his home among the ubiquitous palm trees of Los Angeles.

Introduction

This book offers an unusual—and fun—way to learn over 1,000 SAT-level vocabulary words. Rather than memorize long lists of words with stand-alone definitions, we present here a novel—a mystery—that offers the type of story you would read in your free time. But here, you'll be learning new vocabulary words as you read. Painless!

The SAT has recently undergone a major change, and vocabulary knowledge is more important than ever. Many of the questions on the new Critical Reading and Writing sections depend on your ability to work with unfamiliar words. And with the new Essay requirement, having a strong vocabulary will allow you to write with greater variety.

So, what's the best way to improve your vocabulary? Certainly not trying to memorize lists. You may be able to come up with a one-word definition of *pulchritude* or *deleterious*, but you probably wouldn't be able to understand its broader meaning.

Words should be read in context if you hope to remember them. And that's what this book helps you do. It offers you a way to learn vocabulary words—without the pain of learning them.

There is no way to know precisely which vocabulary words will appear on the SAT. If that were the case, the test would be too predictable. Beware of anyone who declares that certain words appear year after year: Kaplan has analyzed the vocabulary words that appeared on released SATs over the past decade and has come to find out that in fact, no words—except, perhaps, the word *parch*—were more common than others. Having said that, there are types of words—words of medium difficulty, for instance— that high school students are expected to master. The more vocabulary words you learn, the better you'll do on the SAT. And that's what this book is all about.

One of the best ways to learn vocabulary is to learn root words. A *root word* is one to which prefixes (beginnings) and/or suffixes (endings) are added to create different words. All words that share the same root are linked in terms of meaning (though with some words, the root's spelling may change slightly).

Look at the word *carnal*. Unfamiliar? What about *carne*, as in chili con carne? *Carn* means "meat" or "flesh," which leads you straight to the meaning of carnal—pertaining to the flesh. You could decode *carnivorous* ("meat eating") in the same way.

Many words in English come from ancient Greek or Latin root words. When you learn roots, you learn the fundamental bases on which the words were built. Use the Root List at the end of this book to help you learn to decode almost any word.

THE RING
OF McALLISTER

PROLOGUE

A **zephyr** blew gently across the neighborhood, and Will **quivered** at the cool autumn breeze. He shook off the reddish brown and yellow leaves that had fallen from the **deciduous** trees and accumulated against his feet.

His shoulder ached. He wanted to quit *now*. He had asked to stop several times, but Ty kept throwing passes. "Just 'til the streetlights come on," he hollered. Since Ty announced that he was going to play Pop Warner football, Will had dutifully practiced with him every day. Ty was his best friend. It was as simple as that.

Ty had been Will's friend since the first day of kindergarten. Whenever attendance was called, William Lassiter came right before Tyrone Martin. After that, they were always paired together and, in each grade thereafter, seated one behind the other.

The two were destined to be friends. About the same height, they were both smaller than their fourth-grade classmates. Will's two-sizes-too-big clothing—"You'll grow into them," his mother would insist—called attention to his slight frame, and his fair skin contrasted sharply with his dark hair. During cold spells, his cheeks got so red that he appeared to be blushing, which prompted merciless teasing by children and adults alike.

Ty, too, received his fair share of needling, though he was huskier than Will. Saddled with wire-rimmed glasses so ill-fitting that they dwarfed his round olive face, Ty sweetly **deflected** the taunts with his infectious smile.

The football wobbled through the air one last time. Will trapped it in his outstretched arms and hugged the ball close. The ball felt heavier since his last toss. He hesitated.

"Let's practice punting then," called Ty, seeing that his exhausted friend hadn't the **endurance** to throw any longer. "Kick it to me."

Will booted the ball and immediately felt a sting on the top of his foot. While he **grimaced** in pain, the ball sailed past Ty's head and over the gate of the house next door—a derelict property that had stood vacant for years. Bouncing onto the long, **unkempt** driveway, the ball mysteriously picked up speed as it hurled toward the abandoned mansion. Seconds later, it crashed through a window.

Standing at the rusted iron gate, Will and Ty exchanged glances of fear. Although Will was certainly the more **timorous** of the two, he knew he wouldn't be able to **goad** Ty into **retrieving** the ball.

His friend was brave, but not **brazen** enough to go in there. Will would have to get the **errant** ball himself.

In the end, Ty agreed to a compromise. He'd accompany Will to the house, but he refused to go inside. Will was on his own if he wanted to get the football back.

Scaling the fence together, they crept up to the side of the **edifice**. Will **pried** open a weather-beaten French door and looked back at Ty with great reluctance. Ty nodded, **spurring** Will on.

Will found himself in the **solarium**. The ball had crashed through one of the many dirt-encrusted windows of this sunroom. Will located the broken pane and then scanned the room, However, his search proved **futile**; the football was nowhere to be found.

Not wanting to lose the ball, Will considered the alternative. Should he venture farther into the house? As it was, he could barely make out Ty through the **opaque** glass. If he went farther in, he'd really be alone.

Will was **sullen**, torn by his indecision. The football had been a present from his grandfather. Will remembered well the day he had received it. After presenting the gift, the elder Lassiter had promptly **jettisoned** his cane and led Will in a game of catch. In just seconds, he had gone from a **feeble** old man to a sprightly young athlete who threw a ball with **zeal**. A few days later, his grandfather had a stroke. He never recovered.

Will made up his mind to continue the search. Calling out to Ty, he left the **solarium** for the rest of the mansion. Once through the threshold, Will followed a corridor down a flight of stairs, filled with years' worth of dust and cobwebs.

Almost immediately, the temperature seemed to change. Before, Will had felt only a slight chill, but now, he shivered to the bone. Not only that, the **stagnant** air, with its smell of **rancid** decay, was oppressive.

Suddenly, the smell of burning leaves seemed to fill the room, and soon after, a hissing sound. Quiet, almost undetectable at first, it grew to a **crescendo** and then morphed into an eerie, unmistakably maniacal laugh.

Will froze in his tracks. The football could not possibly have carried this far. He turned around and tried to retrace his steps back, but as the sunlight had faded, the staircase was nowhere to be found. Unable to see through the thick darkness, Will grew alarmed, gripped by **claustrophobia**. His heart beat faster, and the **palpitations** only **augmented** his fear that the walls were closing in. He wanted desperately to call to Ty, but the words just wouldn't come out. Terrified, he started running blindly, slamming into walls and tripping over rotted furniture. Finally, he crashed into the fireplace and fell back on the floor, where he lay trembling in the dark.

It was then that Will sensed another presence in the room, an **ominous** spirit **lurking** nearby on the verge of attack. He couldn't make out who it was because of the **paucity** of light. His voice, raspy from weeping, called out.

"Is that you, Ty?"

The ensuing silence crushed any hopes Will had of seeing his friend. Dread set in. He gathered the strength to leap to his feet and stumbled forward, groping around for the doorway. Clutching the doorknob, he rushed into the next room. But as he released the knob, something grabbed him.

A **talon**-like grip pierced Will's arm, reverberating his body with shock. In an instant, a **myriad** of images and sounds flooded his mind, leaving him frozen in time: a woman with an impossibly twisted neck, screams and laughter. Finally, a shadow **obscured** her, and more images—colors really—rushed through him: crimson, orange, magenta, and then gray fading to black.

Just as quickly as it had seized him, the horrific force softened its hold. In a panic, Will struggled violently and tore away, blood oozing from his forearm.

Now the wicked cackle could be heard all around him, as if the house itself were **mocking** him. Will ran from room to room, trying to shake off the laughter, but it gained on him, surrounding him in a maddening **cacophony** of shrieks. Tears began to blur his vision, and soon, he was **hyperventilating**. The stale air was suffocating.

Hopelessly lost and terrified, Will stopped running. He knew he couldn't escape his fate. He closed his eyes, waiting for the phantom to conquer him.

"*Run straight across the hall, Will, and then up the stairs.*"

It was a woman's **dulcet** voice, which both surprised and calmed Will. He opened his eyes, but could see no one. He took a deep breath.

"*The hall, then the stairs. Go. Hurry.*"

Will obeyed. He found the stairs, gripped the banister, and **ascended**. More instructions followed, each in the same sweet voice. Turn right, then left, then down a familiar corridor. Will soon **lumbered** his way back through the vegetation to the French doors. Yet as he turned the handles, he heard that frightening laugh again. And then, a haunting voice whispered, "*Lassiter.*"

With that, Will burst out of the house and collapsed into Ty's arms.

CHAPTER ONE

"Pencils down."

At first, the words didn't register. Will was staring at the scar on his arm, now a glossy shade of peach, his mind too **immersed** in degrees, cosines, and **algorithms** to hear. How could Mrs. O'Leary end 10 months of mathematical torment with such a **laconic** request?

"Pencils down, Mr. Lassiter!"

Her command jolted Will out of his stupor. He put down the pencil, and the world around him gradually came alive. Other students shifted in their seats. Papers rustled. Passing his test booklet to the girl in front of him, Will massaged his throbbing hand and then surveyed the room.

His classmates seemed similarly dazed by the exam. They rubbed their necks, yawned, and stretched their backs. Leave it to

O'Leary to drag the semester to such an **excruciating** end. But at last, that's what it was. The end.

"Have a great summer. See you in September."

Mrs. O'Leary was not given to grand **orations**, though what she said was enough for the weary eleventh graders.

The hallway was littered with crumpled term papers and discarded pens. Overripe gym shorts fell out of lockers that lined the walls. Entire notebooks were now confetti on the floor. Will stepped out into the corridor and was immediately caught in a throng of **exuberant** students making a beeline toward the door.

Outside, Will felt the full force of the sun against his face, the warmth reviving his stiff body. The sun had lightened his hair over the years and tanned his skin to a golden hue. **Casting** a long, thin shadow as he walked, he spotted Ty near a large maple tree.

Ty had grown into a muscular athlete, no longer the small, **pudgy** kid of his youth. Now, nearly half a foot taller than Will, his baby fat was gone, though his round face still wore the same **cherubic** smile.

Standing next to Ty was Katie Watson. Will had known her since the second grade, when they'd both received awards for good citizenship: He'd painted a picture of the town from a bird's-eye view, and Katie had written an **effusive** essay about the importance of community spirit. When they were called up at the awards ceremony, Will's stage fright had overpowered him, and he stood stiffly, admiring Katie's carefree expression. Even now, with her curly scarlet hair and boundless energy, Katie was always in a good mood.

"How'd it go, Will?" Katie could barely contain her enthusiasm that school was finally over.

"I don't know, and I don't care."

Ty rolled his eyes. He knew better.

"I'm sure you aced it."

Will shrugged. Katie snorted impatiently and looped her hands through her friend's arms.

"What are we **loitering** around this place for? Let's get out of here!"

Will and Ty agreed, and Katie led them across the street to Sal's Pizzeria. Even on a hot day, the smell of fresh basil and mozzarella was too intoxicating to pass up.

Housed in an old brick storage warehouse, Sal's was the closest thing to an after-school hangout that this town had. Sal, who practically lived at the pizzeria, was a third-generation restaurateur. Visitors could glimpse his ruddy face every day of the week, **adroitly** tossing dough into the air or mingling with customers. A testament to the quality of his **cuisine**, Sal's **corpulence** had come from years of "sampling." It had gotten to be such a problem that he now had to suck in his gut to pass between the crowded tables. Pizza was in his blood.

Finding a **secluded** table in the back, the three friends attacked their pepperoni pie with gusto. Between mouthfuls, they talked about their plans for the summer.

"I'm gonna sail my butt off so I can beat my brother once and for all," Ty declared.

Will and Katie laughed. Poor Ty. He constantly **vied** for superiority over his older brother Ray. Every year, Ty would pick a new sport. And every year, Ray came out on top. That's not to say Ty was **inept**. Ray was simply the best sailor in Red Fork, as well as the best football player, tennis player, basketball player, and chess player. Where competition was involved, Ray always won.

"Don't you ever get bored sailing around that tiny lake?"

Katie sighed. "Will, don't start that again."

Will wanted to say more, but he **acquiesced**. Ty and Katie were his only friends, and he couldn't afford to **alienate** them. He knew that sooner or later, their differences would divide them. Just not today, not the beginning of summer vacation.

The trio ate in moody silence. When there was only one slice left, they all hesitated, and then simultaneously, reached for it. Their hands smashed together.

"Ty should have it," Will laughed. "He's in training."

The three friends eased back, their exchange falling into a comfortable **ebb** and flow. The summer was panning out in the usual fashion. When he wasn't sailing, Ty would be working at the video store **adjacent** to Sal's. Katie was going to help out at her parents' antique shop. And Will had lined up work as a "landscape engineer," or as Ty **aptly** put it, "a mower of lawns." By the time they rose to leave, the sun had crept into the western horizon.

*   *   *

McAllister Boulevard was the main thoroughfare in the **hamlet** of Red Fork, Pennsylvania. Giant oak trees lined the cobblestone street, providing **perpetual** shade. They were planted a hundred years earlier, back when the town was Algernon McAllister's country estate.

An industrial **magnate**, McAllister **accrued** a fortune in the late nineteenth century building steam engines for locomotives and ships. With his new-found wealth, he was able to buy a large parcel of land outside of Pittsburgh and build Red Fork. His new domain reflected his **patrician** tastes with its **grandiose** mansion and **meticulously** cultivated gardens.

McAllister's estate was so vast that it required its own power plant—steam, of course. He employed a **phalanx** of housekeepers and gardeners, and imported a herd of stallions from the Arabian Peninsula, housing them in spacious stables. McAllister also built the largest private library in the country and his own printing press, with which he planned to publish his memoirs. Unfortunately, he never got the chance.

McAllister died on the maiden voyage of the Titanic. Though he had no heirs, he did leave a will. In it, he specified that Red Fork be split up into equal-sized lots and divided among his loyal servants. This **magnanimous** final gesture secured his place in history as Red Fork's **progenitor** and greatest citizen.

McAllister's story was part of the curriculum at McAllister Elementary School. Fourth graders wrote essays about him and his splendid gift to the town, and sixth graders presented an annual play **depicting** his life. To Will and his friends, it was as legendary a tale as Washington crossing the Delaware.

The three friends strolled along Tess Street until they came upon Algernon Drive. This was Will's block. Ty put his hand on Will's shoulder.

"I'm going for my license in a few weeks. Before you know it, we'll be cruising down McAl' Boulevard. This is going to be our summer."

Will's eyes lit up. "Maybe we can take a road trip—check out the Grand Canyon or something."

"Why?" Ty stared blankly at him. "It's just a big hole in the ground."

Before Will could respond, Ty poked him in the stomach.

"Gotcha!"

Will grinned. "Good one. Remember: Green means go and red means stop, not *go faster*."

"You're one to talk!" Ty **retorted**.

Will backed down. He had taken his driving test twice already and still had only his permit. Parallel parking was the **bane** of his existence. Where in Red Fork would he ever need to parallel park? The one street where people had reason to go, McAllister Boulevard, had diagonal spaces.

Bidding his friends farewell, Will started down Algernon Drive. As he passed the Shaw house, he heard Ty call to him.

"Watch out! Don't let Algie get you!"

To underscore his meaning, Ty let out a series of howls.

The taunt shouldn't have bothered Will. But as his friend's wailing faded, the warning rang loud in Will's head, and he automatically reached down to touch his scar. Edginess overtook him as he walked toward his house. Rounding a bend, Will glanced at the rusted iron gates marking the entrance to Stone Manor, the one-time home of Algernon McAllister.

Stone Manor must have been an impressive sight in its day. Four stories tall with over 40 rooms, the mansion reflected its owner's larger-than-life personality. With its domed roof, the place resembled a medieval cathedral. The **façade** was decorated with sculptures in relief and a colonnade. Named *Stone Manor* because of the Italian marble that once adorned its exterior, the **sobriquet** still applied today, despite the overabundance of moss and ivy that covered the now **dilapidated** shell.

Over the years, "word was" that McAllister's restless spirit haunted the old mansion. People claimed to hear noises

emanating from the house—cries, whispers, and screams. It had been unoccupied for as long as anyone could remember. Even in daylight, there was something menacing about the place. The dark windows seemed to study Will as he passed. He tried to stare back, but quickly lost his nerve.

Will glanced down, tracing the crooked **laceration** on his arm. It brought back memories of that fateful October day seven years ago, though he still wasn't clear about exactly what had happened. His parents had assured him it was all his imagination—that he had probably just taken a bad fall. Ghosts didn't exist. Perhaps, he thought, but there was much **veracity** to the stories about the place—enough for him to believe even now. Unable to **expunge** these thoughts, he started to sprint, running past Stone Manor to his house next door.

Once inside, Will relaxed and resumed his usual course. After dinner and a few hours in front of the television, he went up to his room to sketch.

Will found his bed to be the best spot for drawing, though he knew his mother would complain about the charcoal dust that **accrued** on the comforter. Tonight, he concentrated on a simple **pediment** on the roof of the manor. He drew the triangular gable with the ease that comes from considerable talent. As he sketched, he thought about what Ty had said, that this summer was going to be different because he was getting his driver's license. Will **mused** good-naturedly, *What good does a license do if no one ever wants to go anywhere?*

His eyes suddenly became very heavy, and his breathing slowed. He let the paper and pencil slip from his hand. As he faded to sleep, Will thought he saw an illumination on his globe. Something outside was reflecting off the **orb**. He picked up his head to look out the window: A light from Stone Manor had altered the usually darkened frame. Someone was in there.

CHAPTER TWO

*   *   *

The light came from a window at the heart of the mansion's silhouette. As Will watched, the window seemed to grow in size. Larger and larger, it swelled until Will could see clearly into the house. He suddenly realized that the window had not changed, but that he himself had moved. By some **ethereal** means of **locomotion**, he had floated across the yard from his bedroom into Stone Manor.

But soon, the light **abated**, and in its place came a menacing cloud and **pungent** odor of burning leaves. Will heard a crackle, and turning toward the sound, **discerned** a roaring fireplace through the haze. Will backed away from the heat and fell over a body on the floor. His own body.

Startled, Will leapt to his feet and moved toward the fire, but found that it was no longer there. In its place, a stairwell crept down into darkness. Will started down the steps but could find no landing. He continued, deeper and deeper into the dark abyss. And then he heard the voice: "Lassiter," it breathed.

Will turned to go back up the stairs, but the steps beneath him disappeared. He fell into the darkness, the echoes of that awful laugh ringing all around him....

*   *   *

The high-pitched alarm blared into Will's ears and he bolted upright. His heart pounding, it took him a moment to realize he was in his own bedroom. He glanced out the window at Stone Manor. It looked empty as ever.

Ty and Katie had already started eating when Will finally arrived. He had gone to Sal's first before remembering that Katie had said she was in the mood for burgers. Sprinting along McAllister Boulevard, he'd then cut across the park (whose lawn he had recently seeded) to meet his friends at the Red Fork Café.

The café—a diner really—specialized in comfort food like chicken pot pie, meatloaf, and garlic fries. To Will, though, the **pinnacle** of the culinary experience was the cheddar cheeseburger with onion rings.

He placed his order with Dolores, the owner of the café and Red Fork's leading **curmudgeon**. Not exactly the "hostess with the most-est," she had little patience for those who were indecisive about ordering, and rarely, if ever, bothered to refill the water glasses. Perhaps in her late fifties—no one knew for sure, and no one wanted to ask—Dolores had an unrelenting crankiness that, over the years, had left her face **gnarled** with wrinkles. Her quick temper led her to **admonish** customers regularly, and even to abruptly show a few to the **egress**. Will always knew what he wanted, so he never had any trouble.

He took the seat next to Katie.

"So, have you met your new neighbors yet?"

New neighbors? It took Will a moment to process her **query**. He had assumed that last night's occurrence was all a dream—the stairwell, the floating, and the light in the window. It seemed a more logical explanation than someone actually moving *into* the Manor.

From his silence, Katie gathered that Will didn't know. She explained, "I overheard the butcher's wife tell my mom that she'd been talking to the sheriff who docked his boat next to the real estate agent who told him that someone had bought the manor."

Ty and Will stared blankly at one another after Katie's **convoluted** explanation. A grand example of Red Fork's own version of the Internet, gossip here was more reliable and often faster than its electronic counterpart.

Katie summed up, "But the real question is, who are they?"

Ty suggested that the new owners were vampires, which led to a heated debate between Katie and him over how the bloodsuckers could get approval for a mortgage. As Will listened quietly to their **banter**, Dolores approached the table.

"I heard it was that old movie star," she **opined**. "You know, the one who made all those stupid pictures about cavemen. Joan somebody. She married the guy from that island."

Dolores's grasp of pop culture was about as firm as her scrambled eggs. She had just described an actress who had died more than 30 years ago. But no one was **masochistic** enough to correct her and risk a slew of personal **invectives**.

"Well," she concluded, "Whoever it is, let's hope they last longer than the others."

Dolores didn't need to **elaborate**. Everyone in Red Fork knew about the previous owners of Stone Manor and their tragic ends. There was Algernon McAllister, of course. After him, a gangster named Johnny Gunn bought the place and was **subsequently** killed in a hail of gunfire. Third in ownership was an invalid named Helena Ross. She rolled into Red Fork in the spring of 1953, and within six months, fell headlong to her death down one of the mansion's stairwells.

No one had lived there since Ross. Over time, some had suggested the manor be **razed** and replaced with two or three smaller houses. But there was never serious support for this measure. And Daniel Bell, for one, was thankful for that.

Bell was the **curator** of the local museum and president of the Red Fork Historical Society. An expert in all the **arcane** facts about the town and Algernon McAllister, he just happened to be sitting at the counter.

"They'd better not make any changes over there," he said, as he sipped his soup. He was hunched over the bowl, surrounding it with his free arm as if to protect it from invisible thieves with a **yen** for clam chowder. His balding head glowed in the fluorescent light, and his **rotund** shape spilled over his stool. On this day, as most, Bell sported his signature outfit: a bright red bowtie and matching suspenders. Ty once joked that Bell probably held up his bathing suit with those same support bands.

Through Bell's efforts, Stone Manor had been added to the National Registry of Landmarks. Under "landmark" status, law **precluded** serious modifications, so even though the manor was considered old and **anachronistic** in style, it could only be restored: The new owners would have to **adhere** to its original design.

Ty and Katie had long since polished off the crumbs from their plates when Will swallowed the last bite of his burger. "You guys want to catch a movie or something tonight?"

Katie pursed her lips and sighed. "I've gotta help my parents tally receipts at the store."

"Yeah, no can do, man," Ty weighed in. "I'm meeting Ray at the lake to get some sailing practice in."

Will smiled **wryly**, "Guess I'm on my own then."

After saying their good-byes, Will started to walk aimlessly and replayed the lunch conversation in his head. In the face of Ty and Katie's easy exchange, Will couldn't help but feel that he was becoming more and more **disengaged** from his friends. A division seemed to be mounting between them, which made Ty and Katie different somehow and less **accessible** to him. Today, however, that wasn't of **paramount** concern: The confirmation that someone had indeed moved into Stone Manor was.

Will wondered how much of the previous night was real and how much was a dream. The **vivid** imagery returned: His **aerial** passage across the back garden, the sight of his own body lying on the floor, and the stairway with no landing. While the scenes themselves were clear enough, their meaning remained **cryptic**, and at a loss for how to interpret them, Will put them out of his mind.

Will's wanderings took him from the café through the business district and then past the **arboretum**, where the tallest and oldest of the many oak trees in Red Fork resided. By the time he returned home, he had traversed much of the small town without so much as breaking a sweat.

*   *   *

Will stayed in his room until his mother called him down for dinner. Computer solitaire and Beatles music were keeping him sufficiently entertained. The Fab Four had been his favorite group ever since he could remember: When he was three, Will used to dance with his mother to the upbeat *A Hard Day's Night*, and as he got older, he came to appreciate the group's more **subtle** and sophisticated works. Even today, his eyes misted over every time he heard the **poignant** "Eleanor Rigby."

Joining his parents in the kitchen, Will picked at the fresh trout his father had grilled. Like his son, Ken Lassiter was slim, though he'd long ago outgrown the gawkiness that now afflicted Will. Ken was very comfortable in his body, and it showed in his expressiveness as a teacher at the middle school. A literary **zealot**, he taught his class passionately, engaging his students with absorbing reenactments of Edgar Allan Poe's "The Tell-Tale Heart" and Mark Twain's *The Adventures of Tom Sawyer*. During the summers, he pursued his hobbies with the same **vim**, tackling a different project each year. Last year, it was carpentry; he and Will built a sturdy deck in the back of the house. This year, it was cooking, and as the summer was just starting, Ken had a long way to go before mastering the culinary arts. Tonight's trout, for example, had been marinated in an odd mixture of pineapple juice, dill, and cayenne pepper, and then grilled about 20 minutes too long.

Will sighed as he separated the scales from the charred filet. The unlikely combination of flavors, coupled with his **aversion** to fish, made Will yearn for a **succulent** burger.

"Mmmm!" Will's mother, Joanne, looked up at Ken with a forced smile. Her eyes tearing over from the pepper, "Delicious, honey."

High school sweethearts, Will's parents married the day after graduation. Joanne, also a teacher, had been impressing the value of an arts education on fourth graders for nearly 20 years. Will had inherited her ivory **pallor**, but not her wavy blond hair or deep blue eyes. Joanne was actually a smidge taller than Ken, which never ruffled any feathers in the marriage, though it did discourage her from wearing high-heeled shoes.

Not much bigger than a cottage, their house had been in Ken's family since the creation of the town. The living room, kitchen, and den were on the first floor, with the two small bedrooms upstairs. In fact, it had originally served as the quarters of Algernon McAllister's head servant and personal valet—who, as it turns out, was none other than Ken's grandfather and Will's great-grandfather.

What the house lacked in size, it made up for in warmth. Joanne had **imbued** the home with a lively sense of nature. She painted idyllic **tableaux** of geese in flight and babbling brooks directly onto the walls, creating the impression that the rooms were larger than they really were. She also collected figurines and placed them throughout the house. Will frequently discovered tiny new statues poking out from bookcases and shelves. He found them comforting—miniature friends looking out for him.

Finishing his last bite of trout, Will spotted a small stack of envelopes on the chair next to him, and as he sorted through the mail, snatched out the two letters addressed to him. They were both from colleges: New York University and University of Virginia. He had requested brochures from the two schools. Ken noticed the glossy magazine-like flyers, glanced at Joanne, and sighed.

"You know, McAllister College has a great curriculum and top-notch professors. Your mother and I went there."

Well, that was quick, Will thought. It usually took a few minutes of "We love you" and "We want you to be happy" before one of his parents mentioned McAllister College. There was nothing wrong with the school—it was just that if Will ended up there, he'd feel as though he were in thirteenth grade. Half his classmates **matriculated** there, the rest skipping college to get jobs around town.

McAllister College had been endowed by its namesake in his will, and as such, was practically free for Red Fork residents. There were no dorms, since most students lived at home. Will knew that his parents didn't earn a lot, and he was sure he could qualify for financial aid and perhaps even win a scholarship. He said as much to his parents.

"It's not a question of money, Will," was his father's response.

And with that, Will took the offensive. "Then what's it a question of?"

Now he had them. There was no way they could argue their way out of it.

"We just want you to stay close to home. We worry. That's what parents do."

Will rolled his eyes in **exasperation**. His mother's **plaintive** comment drove home the rules of this debate, and they did not favor him. His father went in for the kill.

"Maybe after a couple of years, you could transfer—"

"Just forget it!"

Will bolted from his chair and stormed up to his room, slamming the door behind him. He was seeing red, and he leaned against the door for a moment, trying to calm down. His father's words echoed in his ears. If they wouldn't let him attend the college of his choice now, how would two years change their minds? *Why are they holding me back?* Frustrated, Will grabbed a half-finished sketch, and ripped it to shreds.

An hour later, his father knocked on his door. They were going to catch a movie and wanted Will to go. Ken's voice was bright and **conciliatory**.

Will faked a loud yawn. "I think I'll turn in early."

The truth was, he was wide awake, but so angry he couldn't stand to be around them.

*   *   *

The house was still. Will had been alone for a few hours, and the relative quiet relaxed him. The only sound he could **discern** was the relentless twittering of a cricket outside. He went to his window to confront the offending pest but instead found himself the subject of two piercing eyes—the two lit windows in the manor. The **behemoth** seemed ready to devour him. Will blinked and tried to refocus.

A strong breeze blew through the side yard, driving the clothesline into a series of **torsions**. The still-moist sheets twisted furiously on the rope. Turning away from the window, Will retreated to his bed, though the creaks from downstairs and the clanking storm door unsettled him.

A while later, the gust died down and the noises fell silent. The cricket, however, persisted in his chatter. This time, though, Will found the **sonorous** chirps soothing. But as he settled back and turned on the television, there was one more loud noise: *Tap-tap*. Someone was knocking at the front door.

Will held his breath. Not wanting to reveal himself, he **surreptitiously** crept to the top of the stairs, and tried to make out who or what was down there. No luck. As he **deliberated** about what to do, there was another, more insistent rap. Will exhaled slowly and descended the stairs, **warily** opening the door.

"Is this yours?"

A beautiful young woman held out a tattered football.

Will studied her. With high cheekbones that drew attention to her hazel eyes and long brown hair cascading down her back, she was the most stunning girl Will had ever seen. Not only that, but her voice, songlike and affectionate, was a **tonal** déjà vu for him: He was sure he'd heard her before. And with the way she stared back at him, Will could swear she felt the same way. For an instant, Will was transported back to the day when he, as a small boy, was trapped in Stone Manor: She sounded just like the mysterious woman who had guided him to safety. But what was that same apparition doing on his front porch?

"I didn't mean to alarm you. I'm Laura. My dad and I just moved in next door."

Moved in next door? She was real?

"William Lassiter, right?"

Laura showed him the dusty ball. Just below the stitches, Will's name was still **legible** in faded magic marker. His grandfather had written it there.

"You're a man of few words, William."

"W-w-Will."

Laura smiled.

"I guess we're neighbors, Will."

She waited for a response, but none was forthcoming. Between the unsettling wind, the familiar voice, and the memories awakened by the football, Will couldn't think straight enough to muster chitchat with the attractive girl standing in front of him. He tried to **conjure** up a **suave** comment, but before he could open his mouth, a man's voice boomed with authority.

"Laura! It's getting late. Come inside."

She flipped the football to Will. "That's my dad. I gotta go. See ya."

As Will juggled it for control, she spun around. He corralled the **wayward** ball and watched as she **sauntered** across the lawn. Apparently, Will had just met Stone Manor's new owner.

CHAPTER THREE

The sun was still low in the sky, but already much was going on next door. After tossing and turning all night, Will stumbled out of bed and over to the window to investigate the commotion. Laura and her father were tossing a **bevy** of broken tables and other assorted junk into a newly parked dumpster in their driveway. Apparently, one of the lesser-known legends about Stone Manor concerned the sheer number of useless items that had accumulated there.

Will stood transfixed as Laura and her father paraded out several moldy chairs, a cracked vase, a rusted birdcage, and a crumbling armoire. The **penultimate** of these objects, the birdcage, looked especially intriguing, as though it had housed a canary or other small bird. Will recalled stories he had read about how coal miners used canaries to make sure the caves they were in had not collapsed. As long as the canary sang, the coal miners knew that the passage was clear. With a **morbid** curiosity, Will squinted to see whether the cage contained any bird remains.

His hair still disheveled from the restless night, Will stood glued to the scene. Again and again, his eyes came back to Laura— Laura pulling a decrepit trunk out the front door, Laura hauling a pile of old clothing down the driveway, Laura and her father pushing a moth-infested rug over the six-foot, **corrugated** steel walls of the dumpster. She'd tucked her long tresses under a baseball cap, but a few tendrils had managed to escape. Her sleeveless shirt and cut-off shorts accentuated her slim form, and Will admired Laura's bare and well-toned arms. Despite the rigors of her labor, Will could tell from her animated gestures to her father that Laura was **ebullient**, and Will was intrigued. As she walked to and from the manor, her graceful **gait** mesmerized him.

Reminded of her casual exit the night before, Will glanced away, recalling too his own aloofness and lack of **eloquence**. *You were real slick*, he **chided** himself, ashamed. Looking up at her distant figure again, he **resolved**, *Next time. Next time, I'll keep my wits about me.*

As it turned out, Will wasn't the only one spying on the new residents of Red Fork. Passing cars slowed down, and neighbors gathered in front on the sidewalk. With each trip inside, the pair carted out busted lamps, shattered mirrors, and corroded furniture. The onlookers marveled at the seemingly **interminable** energy of father and daughter as they cleaned out the mansion.

When Laura waved to the crowd, a few of the ordinarily **reticent** neighbors returned the gesture. Most just whispered among themselves. Clearly, the newcomers were the talk of the town.

It wasn't long before Daniel Bell arrived on the scene. Emerging from his car, Bell called out, "Dr. Perez?" Laura's father met him halfway down the driveway. From where he was standing, Will couldn't hear much more of the conversation, but it seemed that Bell was, like everyone else, curious and apprehensive. Will **surmised** he was there to make sure nothing of historical interest was being thrown away.

Dr. Perez led Bell to the dumpster and pointed at the various contents. Bell nodded, and the two men shared a laugh, moving to sort through some plates and other pieces of china. With a nod from Perez, Bell selected a few pieces and put them in a box, which he proceeded to move to the car. Just as he opened the door, Laura ran over holding a pile of yellowed newspapers. Bell looked ecstatic as he **perused** and eagerly accepted the old papers. Now he had even more **artifacts** for the museum. He shook Dr. Perez's hand again, this time pumping his arm excitedly, then drove off.

Satisfied that Bell had approved of Stone Manor's new owner, the townspeople followed suit and began to **disperse**. Will left his window to shower and get ready for work.

Since he didn't yet have his driver's license, Will had to walk around town with his mower in tow. So before he left home, he had to be sure that everything was in perfect running order. He checked the lawn mower blades for wear, brushed the air filter, and filled the tank with gas. Balancing a five-gallon jug of extra fuel on top of the engine, he set out for Monday's clients.

His first customers, the Huffmans, lived around the block on Oakton Street. Will pushed the mower along the uneven sidewalk, frequently stopping to **disengage** the undercarriage from tree roots that broke through the surface of the aged cement. At last, Will arrived at his destination and surveyed the property.

He noted the two birch trees near the mailbox and the marigolds growing alongside the front of the house. These would prove tricky to **circumnavigate** with his bulky mower. Will left the machine in the driveway while he walked on the lawn, feeling for depressions in the ground. He squatted down and scanned the line of the property, identifying the slight upgrade that sloped toward the east. Will treated every lawn with this same **scrutiny**. His reason for this became clear as soon as he started to work.

Will yanked the cord on the mower, and the engine roared to life. He began near the fence and worked his way toward the driveway, mowing not in straight lines but a series of gentle curves. The **serpentine** lines he created seemed random at first. Pivoting, he changed direction, cutting the lawn at an angle almost perpendicular to his previous course. He swerved, backed up at various points, and then employed a set of quick-turn maneuvers.

To an **idle** observer, Will's strategy was inefficient, if not plain crazy. But as the end result would prove, there was more than method to his "madness"—there was inspiration. For Will combined his **penchant** for drawing with his summer profession: He treated the lawns as large canvases, using the natural grain of the land to reproduce works of art he had seen in his mother's books. Gradually, the **ambiguous** design he was carving in the grass became the familiar and **enduring** portrait of the *Mona Lisa*.

Will wiped away the beads of sweat that had formed on his forehead and then admired his handiwork. *Her smile was easier this time*, he thought. *I'm getting better at this.* He took a swig from his water bottle and then knocked on the front door.

Mrs. Huffman met him at the **ingress** and ran her eyes over Will's creation. Will said nothing, believing the work spoke for itself. He was correct.

"The *Mona Lisa*. Again. That's ... nice," she said, biting her lower lip.

Mrs. Huffman retreated through the front doors and returned with his payment and a glass of lemonade. Will walked over to one of the birch trees and plopped down on the newly cut grass, leaning against the trunk. The Huffman's garage opened and a black BMW rolled onto the driveway. Brady, a classmate from school, was at the wheel. Craning his neck to see the lawn, Brady's eyes settled **dubiously** on Will. He shook his head in **disbelief** and, just loud enough for Will to hear, muttered, "Freak." Gunning the engine, he peeled out of the driveway and tore down the block.

Will watched as the car zipped away. With a twinge of regret, he remembered the friendship they'd shared in elementary school, attending three of Brady's birthday parties and playing soccer together in the street along with Ty and Katie. Brett, Richie, Erica, Ryan, Max, and Sue had also played. They had all been friends … but that was years ago. Now, with the exception of Ty and Katie, it seemed none of them wanted anything to do with Will.

There was no incident he could recall, no blow-out that had severed their friendship. It had merely come about after Will told Brady about his experience inside Stone Manor. Brady had been **incredulous**, and didn't believe that Will, of all people, would have the courage to enter the desolate place. After that, news spread that Will had **prevaricated** the whole story, and one by one, his friends stopped calling. By the time they reached middle school, Ty and Katie were the only kids who dared to be seen sitting next to him at lunch.

Nowadays, Will came across his former friends only when he bumped into them in the hallway, or at times like these when he mowed their parents' lawns. All in all, their exchanges were about as **verbose** and kind as Brady's. Will had long ago accepted his status as class **pariah**. But still, he hated to be reminded of it.

Will had a light schedule—only five lawns—and he took his time doing them to keep from getting sunstroke. He stopped frequently to **hydrate** himself, drinking more than a gallon of water over the course of the day. By the time the sun began to set,

Will had completed a Monet, a Cézanne, and a Rembrandt. His final masterpiece, an abbreviated version of *Dogs Playing Poker*, drew **kudos** from his client, who just happened to own a bloodhound, two beagles, and a fox terrier.

Night came, and with it, the **incandescent** glow of fireflies. Fireflies appeared only in the warm weather, so their arrival was always a **harbinger** of summer. They skittered through the air, a swarm of **diminutive** lights illuminating Will as he pushed his mower up his driveway.

A weary Will **ascended** the stairs to his room. He put the day's **remuneration** in a manila envelope on his desk, and sat down, intent on drawing, but like an involuntary reflex, he had to check on Stone Manor. He was no longer surprised by the lights in the mansion, but tonight something else captured his attention.

It was unmistakably Laura. Arms outstretched, she was hanging a picture on the wall in what Will assumed was her room. She stepped back to examine the frame and then adjusted a crooked corner. Will continued to watch as she moved about, unloading knick-knacks from boxes and placing them on her dresser. Embarrassed that he was spying on her, Will looked away, but then couldn't help but turn back. But this time, when he fixed his eyes on her, he froze: Laura was facing him, staring back. She lifted her hand and waved.

Immediately, Will ducked below his desk. Mortified that she caught him, he crawled along the floor to the opposite side of the room toward the light switch. His face burned with embarrassment. *How long did she see me watching her?* Before he could **fathom** a guess, though, he realized something far more important ... and intriguing: Laura had been looking at him. Will's eyes widened with excitement, and he sprang up and darted across the room to return the wave. He reached the casement and stuck his head outside, but she was no longer there.

A sense of relief draped over him. Will had no idea what he would have said or done beyond wave, and now the decision had been made for him. He climbed into bed blissfully content that Laura had been watching him and drifted off to sleep.

*　*　*

Laura came to the window again, her auburn hair glistening in the moonlight. She waved to him, then pivoted out of sight, her long tresses swaying against her back. A shadowy figure moved across the window, following her. Will opened his mouth to scream a warning but he couldn't make a sound. In silent horror, he watched as Laura's room plunged into darkness.

CHAPTER FOUR

The following morning, there would be no artwork on the lawn. Will was too preoccupied to fashion any pictures on his front yard, and instead, pushed the mower back and forth in standard parallel lines. He rarely—if ever—had nightmares, and now, in the span of three nights, he'd had two. The memory of a dark form trailing Laura was haunting him. And just as he was imagining an outstretched arm about to grab her, something pulled at his shoulder.

Will wheeled around to find Laura standing behind him and jumped back, alarmed by her sudden physical appearance. Surprised at his reaction, she aped his expression and then laughed.

"You're wound tight." She stuffed her hands in her pockets and smiled shyly. Her **composure** was more mannered today, but it was welcoming enough to disarm Will. After a brief, awkward silence, Laura continued. "I was just bored and thought I'd come over to see what's doing...." Her voice trailed off as she tugged her thumbs through the belt loop of her shorts.

Laura seemed unusually nervous to Will. In their past encounters, she seemed so self-assured and easygoing. *Of course*, it dawned on him, *I've already snubbed her twice. She's probably reacting to my* **reticence**. His eyes fell to the ground, and he blushed at his social **ineptness**. *Well*, he raised his head to gaze at her, *this is the second chance I've been waiting for.* "You know—" He stopped to clear his throat. "I've got just one more lawn to do, and it can wait...." *So far, so good.* "And I was thinking, maybe I could show you around town?" His voice cracked on the last syllable, but at least he'd gotten it all out.

Laura's radiant smile **presaged** her response. "That'd be great!" Her confident and cheery tone had returned, and she cocked her head, beaming, "It's about time I learned my way around." Her enthusiasm bolstered him, and he grinned back.

"Awesome," said Will. But with his newfound confidence, he couldn't leave well enough alone. "Do you mind waiting a bit? I just want to finish this lawn—I don't like to leave a job half-done."

"No problem," Laura **acceded**, "that's a good policy." She was still smiling as she tucked her hair behind her ear. "Very **conscientious**." She was babbling now. "Do you need a hand?"

Realizing they both had a **plethora** of nervous energy that could lead to hours of incoherent **prattle**, Will simply nodded.

Laura exhaled, grateful and relieved that their initial awkwardness had finally passed. She immediately went for the electric edger, which she used to trim the grass along the driveway. Monitoring her progress from the lawn, Will was surprised to see how **dexterous** she was. In a short time, the chore was completed and they set out for their expedition.

From Algernon Drive, Will guided Laura to the left and they headed north on Tess Street. First, they passed a large Tudor-style home that Will explained was the "laundry house," the maids' quarters on the original Red Fork property. In addition to living there, the maids had washed the clothes and linens for the entire estate on these premises.

To underscore his point, Will glanced at the enormous vats alongside the house. Turning to follow his gaze, Laura raised her hand to shield her eyes from the bright sunlight, revealing a small **contusion** on her right temple.

"Ow, that looks like it hurts."

"Oh," Laura ran her fingers over the bruise. "It's nothing. I'm a total klutz." She rolled her eyes, blushing. "I fell down some steps this morning."

Will immediately remembered Helena Ross and her fatal fall. He opened his mouth to share the story, but he thought the better of it and clamped his lips shut. He didn't want to scare Laura with the tragic tale.

They soon came upon a row of attached houses. The ruddiness of the red brick construction was **tempered** by the gray slate roof. These had been McAllister's stables. Converted into individual dwellings after his death, they were now occupied by Red Fork residents—Katie and her family among them. Each house had high ceilings and a loft **accessible** by spiral staircase. Laura was impressed.

"This reminds me of an artists' colony I once visited in France."

Will was **riveted**. "You've been to France?"

"I went with my parents when I was ten," Laura shrugged **nonchalantly**. "We also saw England, Spain, and Portugal. My father was researching the lives of European explorers." She paused, her eyes developing a faraway glaze. "That was the last trip we took with my mom. She was diagnosed with cancer soon after we got back." Laura pursed her lips. "She died a few months later."

A heavy silence followed. Laura stared at the pavement as they walked, and Will struggled to piece together words of condolence. Before he could offer his sympathies, Laura turned to him shyly.

"I'm sorry. I didn't mean for that to come out. It's just that ever since she died, my dad and I have moved around a lot. I guess I really haven't been able to talk to anyone about it. I mean," she gestured between them, "you know, to people my own age. It's hard to make lasting friendships when...."

She shrugged helplessly, and her voice trailed off. Will could see that she needed his encouragement to continue, so he **obliged** gently. He **broached** the subject of her other travels.

"Tell me about the places you've been."

Laura smiled appreciatively and launched into her experiences moving with her father from Arizona to Chicago and then to Red Fork. When she started to describe Chicago, Will excitedly cut her off.

"Did you go to the Art Institute?"

"Of course."

"So you saw *Sunday*—"

"*Afternoon on the Island of La Grande Jatte*?" Laura filled in the rest of his question and grinned. "Yup, I've seen it a bunch of times."

Will knew the painting from one of his art books. The artist, Georges Seurat, had painted an enormous **panorama** using a technique known as *pointillism*. He created his shapes not with traditional brush strokes, but by applying groups of **miniscule** dots to a blank canvas. When viewed from a distance, these tightly packed **motes** formed the figures in the scene.

"Wow," Will marveled. "I've only seen it in books."

"You've got to see it in person—to stand in front of it, up close. Then you really appreciate what Seurat was able to do."

Will knew Laura was right. *Someday*, he thought, *someday, I will.*

As they walked on, Laura continued to **extol** the many merits of the Windy City—the Loop, Wrigley Field, and sunrises on Lake Michigan.

They reached the end of Tess Street and turned west onto Rufus Drive. Rufus, Will **elucidated**, had been McAllister's father and Tess his mother, hence the street names.

"Roo-fus, eh?" Laura snorted sarcastically. "With a name like that, *Algernon* was doomed right from birth."

Her **wry** wit caught Will off guard, and he laughed heartily.

They **rambled** down Rufus Drive, passing a large **equestrian** field that had once played host to McAllister's storied polo matches but now lay **fallow**. Will pointed out that despite the natural fertilizer provided by the horses, the land was not **arable**. Eventually, they reached the slow-moving Fox River, turned onto Riverview Avenue, and traveled alongside the **languid** water.

As they headed south, Will recalled fishing on this shore with his father and grandfather. "My grandfather was an expert fly fisherman," Will boasted. "But my dad never caught on." He **scoffed** at the memory. "Whenever he **cast** the line, he always swung too low, and the hook ended up getting caught on the back of his collar."

Laura laughed, visualizing the scene. "So your family is pretty close-knit?"

"Oh yeah," Will enthused. "Four generations have lived here in Red Fork, so I was practically raised by my grandparents, aunts and uncles, and my older cousin." He paused, recalling his family history. "My great-grandfather, Henry Lassiter, was McAllister's personal butler, and on my mother's side, my great-grandfather was one of the groomsmen in the stables." Will's **discourse** flowed effortlessly, now that he was growing more comfortable around Laura.

"Wow, I never even knew my grandparents," Laura paused thoughtfully. "I would have liked to...." Her voice was soft. Presently, she straightened up and looked at Will. "Neither of my parents knew much of their **lineage**." She chuckled, "It's **ironic**, my dad being a historian and all."

As they approached the **arboretum**, Will guided Laura to a path that traversed the wooded area. Along the trail, they saw signs identifying the **variegated** flowers and other colorful **flora**. Squirrels and other **arboreal** creatures **cavorted** in the branches of the oak trees. When Will pointed up at a blue jay's nest, Laura noticed the long scar on his arm. "Yikes! Where did you get that?" She reached up to move her fingers over it.

Before she could touch it, Will pulled his arm away and forced a casual tone. "This little scratch? When I was a kid. Football injury."

Laura raised an eyebrow questioningly, "Football, eh?"

Loath to **elaborate**, Will nodded toward the ground. "Hey, look, rabbit tracks!" he chirped lamely.

Noting how sensitive Will was on the subject, Laura obediently gazed at the imprints and pursued the topic no more.

Next came the business district. Passing the movie theater, the supermarket, Sal's, and the video store, the pair strolled along the main street, where Will was greeted by various townsfolk. Red Fork was, after all, a small town. Eventually, they arrived at the cemetery. "Just about everyone who's ever lived in Red Fork is buried here," said Will matter-of-factly. "My family's plot is right over there." He pointed to a small enclosure.

Laura studied the etched tombstones thoughtfully. She turned away from the gray markers and lifted her head to meet Will's eyes. Her voice was uneasy, "Do you mind if we get out of here?" With that, she started ahead.

"Yeah, sure!" Will's bright voice hid his **chagrin**. *Nice going,* he **chided** himself, *can you be any more gruesome?*

Just past the cemetery stood Town Hall. Dwarfed only by Stone Manor, Town Hall had been the estate guesthouse. A mansion in its own right, it housed all the local government offices as well as the motor vehicle bureau and the jail. You could **legislate** leash laws for cats, get married, obtain a fishing license, change your license plates, and file for unemployment all on the same floor.

Crossing the street, they came upon a small two-story house that had originally been where the gatekeeper lived. Though the actual property had extended another mile or so to the east, this structure marked the official entrance to the estate. Today, it was home to the Red Fork Historical Society and self-described **chronicler** of the town, Daniel Bell. Peering through a window, Will and Laura found Daniel busily labeling the objects he had collected from Stone Manor.

Across the park, they stopped to inspect the bronze statue of Algernon McAllister. His arms outstretched to encompass his property, McAllister's 10-foot frame towered over them. He was outfitted in the traditional garb of a gentleman from his time: tailored pants and a knee-length top coat obscuring his buttoned vest and upturned shirt collar. His pose **exuded** an aura of authority and power, and Laura dropped her eyes to read the quote inscribed at the base. "May this **largess** to my servants grant to them and their **posterity** a life filled with peace and prosperity." Laura raised her eyes to the **imposing** character again, impressed. Nearby, two small children swung on a jungle gym under the watchful eyes of their mother.

Will stopped and turned to Laura. "If we keep going on McAllister Boulevard," he gestured down the road, "We'll hit the college and then the interstate a few miles later." He added, "It's the only road out of town."

Laura, meanwhile, was basking in the **serenity** of her surroundings. "I really like it here," she said wistfully. "There's a real neighborly, supportive feel to this place I haven't had in a really long time. We've moved around so much, I was thinking I'd always have to live out of a suitcase."

Will smiled encouragingly, but inside his stomach dropped. The very sense of unity that she was admiring was just the thing that was stifling him. Red Fork was **insular**, removed from the rest of the world. Laura had lived the life Will wanted for himself, and he ached to share his feelings of **claustrophobia** with her. But he held his tongue: This was the beginning of what he hoped was a friendship, and he didn't want to **estrange** Laura.

Back on Tess Street, they stepped inside an antique store to meet Katie and her parents. The store housed an **eclectic** array of artwork, furniture, and figurines. Balancing an armful of boxes, Ty greeted them at the door. He was helping Katie's father transfer some inventory from the basement.

"It's you!" Katie surprised face emerged from behind the counter.

Laura looked questioningly at Will, and he blushed a deep shade of crimson.

Katie smiled in welcome. "You're the girl who moved into Stone Manor, right?"

Will exhaled, relieved that the rumor mill Katie subscribed to had not yet learned of his infatuation with Laura. Of course, that didn't prevent Ty from stirring up trouble.

"So, what do you think of our boy Will?" Ty addressed Laura and clapped Will loudly on the shoulder. "He's a real rebel without a cause, eh?"

Ty snickered at his **sardonic** reference to Will's withdrawn **demeanor**. Will turned uneasily to Laura but found her admiring an **ornate** lamp. *Maybe she didn't hear,* he hoped lamely. Aloud, he said, "Well, we'd better go."

They left the store and walked in silence until they arrived at Stone Manor. Convinced that Laura had indeed picked up on Ty's remark, Will shuffled his feet, hands jammed into pockets. "I guess I'll see you la—"

Laura whirled around. "Yeah, thanks for showing me around. It was fun." Crossing her arms, she added hesitantly, "Hey, do you wanna come over?"

Will's eyes lit up, and he followed her through the open gates.

CHAPTER FIVE

No sooner had they stepped through the gates than Will's exhilaration turned to dread. The **august** mansion loomed large in front of them, and Will was unsettled that Laura might ask him in. The prospect of revisiting the place sent a shiver through his body. Just when he'd made up his mind to tell Laura he couldn't stay after all, she pointed ahead of them.

"There's my father."

Will looked up to see a distinguished man approaching them. Tall and with a hint of gray in his well-groomed beard, Dr. Perez smiled **congenially** and held out his hand. Will shook it and introduced himself. On hearing the name, Dr. Perez nodded in recognition.

"Ah, the football player," he said with a slight Spanish accent.

Quick to correct Dr. Perez, Will stuttered, "A-actually, I'm not—"

"I used to play baseball myself," Dr. Perez beamed. "I had to give it up, though, when I learned I couldn't hit the curve ball." With that, Perez produced a cheerful laugh. His **jocular** manner, much like his daughter's, immediately set Will at ease.

"Laura tells me you're a historian. Do you specialize in any particular **genre**?"

From the older man's pleased **countenance**, Will could see that Perez appreciated his attempt to make conversation.

"I myself am fascinated by the *conquistadors*," Dr. Perez **articulated** the word in its true Spanish pronunciation. "They were adventurers from Spain who explored and **exploited** the New World."

"He's written a few books about them," Laura bragged. "There was even a special on PBS."

Will studied Dr. Perez carefully. There was something familiar about him. "Is your first name Octavio?" Will asked.

Dr. Perez expressed surprise, and Will realized that he knew him, or at least, knew of him. "I think I read something you wrote in *National Geographic*. About the Moors and their castles."

"In Spain, yes." Dr. Perez smiled broadly with a new respect for Will. "I'm impressed someone your age has such a **keen** interest in history." He shot Laura a knowing glance. "You see, not everyone buys it just for the pictures."

Truth be told, Will's primary reason for getting the magazine *was* for the pictures—he liked to sketch reproductions of the stunning images. But in this case, because he was captivated by faraway places, he actually had read the accompanying text.

Dr. Perez continued eagerly, "If you'd like, I've written an entire book about the Moors."

Laura stepped in on Will's behalf. "That's not a book, Dad. It's a **tome**." She held her thumb and forefinger wide apart to indicate its thickness.

Will resorted to a bit of **diplomacy**. "Sure, I'd like to see it." Not wanting Octavio to think him a **laggard**, or Laura to think he was kissing up to her father, Will made a point of making his answer both sincere and vague. And then quickly changed the subject. "What brings you to Red Fork?"

Perez gestured to the house. "The man himself: Algernon McAllister. I'm researching his life for one of my books. When I heard that his home was for sale, I couldn't pass up the opportunity. To live in Stone Manor, sleeping in the same room," Dr. Perez's eyes narrowed, hungrily, "Taking in the same sights, breathing the same air…. Naturally, I jumped at the chance."

Will thought it was anything but natural to want to live in the place, but he understood Dr. Perez's meaning. This was his method of study, to get as close as possible to his subject. And it was why he'd dragged Laura and her mother all over the globe. By Will's estimate alone, they'd lived in at least five different houses scattered across three countries.

Dr. Perez squatted to sit on the front steps, and Will joined him there, thankful they hadn't moved indoors. Settling onto the marble stoop, his eyes followed the column next to him, up to the rafters where it supported a **rococo** frieze **depicting** the Trojan War. This was the closest he'd been to the mansion since his childhood incident.

Almost as if he'd read Will's mind, Octavio brought up Stone Manor. "This place has quite a history, doesn't it?"

Will shifted uneasily.

"Algernon McAllister, Johnny Gunn, Helena Ross. Sad stories."

At least the realtor was honest with him before they moved in, Will thought.

"But what's more intriguing are the rumors," Dr. Perez continued. "Like Johnny Gunn's gold statue."

Will nodded, "I've heard of that one. Gunn had a gold statue—only it wasn't a statue. It was a showgirl who he'd caught cheating on him with a musician. As revenge, he drowned her in gold."

Dr. Perez raised an eyebrow. "A dramatic end, no?" He paused for effect. "That's the popular version, but it's **apocryphal**. You see, when Gunn 'bought the farm'—bang, bang, bang," Dr. Perez chuckled at himself, "the police then raided the manor and found a statue. But it wasn't gold—just gold paint. And it wasn't a woman underneath, it was a mannequin!" He laughed at the absurdity of it. "So, Will, what other stories have you heard?"

Glancing at his sneakers, Will paused. What could he **recount** that wouldn't frighten them? He rummaged through all the horror stories until he remembered a small, **inoffensive** item. "McAllister's ring," he croaked.

"What's that?" Laura and her father chimed in unison.

Will stammered, "Well, apparently, he had this big ring." He searched his mind for more details. "There were loads of diamonds on it. It must have been worth a fortune. After he died, people looked all over the mansion but couldn't find it." Will fell silent, hoping his tale would be sufficient. It was a good, safe **anecdote**, nothing scary or even mildly **lurid**. Just a little story about a piece of jewelry.

But Dr. Perez was **enthralled**. "I never read anything about a ring," he boomed. "What a great symbol of McAllister's **opulence**. It's probably with him at the bottom of the Atlantic."

"Yeah, that's what you'd think. But people still talk about it today. You know," Will's eyes widened comically, **mocking** the significance, "The Ring of McAllister!"

Dr. Perez was amused by Will's **jaded** comment. He stroked his beard thoughtfully. "Tales of fabulous treasures lost … still waiting to be discovered. It's powerful stuff—the stuff of legends."

"And then there's the granddaddy legend of them all," Laura chirped. "That Stone Manor is *haunted*." She grinned half-heartedly, and shot a look at Will. "What do you think? You live next door. Ever seen anything strange over—"

"No," Will **proclaimed** too loudly, suddenly fixated on an invisible piece of lint on his shirt. Quieting his tone, "Of course not."

Dr. Perez examined Will curiously for a moment. "So you make nothing of those stories about children disappearing over the years?"

Will's shrug was unconvincing. "That's just something our parents told us as kids to scare us off, keep us off the property. You know, for our own safety. There's a lot of broken glass, rotted stairs and stuff." His voice cracked. "Someone could have gotten hurt." He peered at Laura and Dr. Perez, willing them to buy his story.

Laura **pondered** his explanation, and her initially **skeptical** expression gradually dissolved into a look of understanding. "Yeah, I guess almost every small town has a 'haunted' house."

Will exhaled a sigh of relief. "Yeah," he added, "What's up with that?"

Dr. Perez **chortled**, "I suppose it makes towns seem more worldly, more **cosmopolitan**." He stood up and stretched his back. "Well, time to get back to work." Glancing at Laura, "You coming, my dear?"

She paused, pouting, before nodding her **assent**.

"Oh," Dr. Perez turned to Will. "That reminds me. Laura tells me you're the best landscaper in Red Fork. Are you interested in taking on a little project?" He waved his hand at the vast territory around the house. What had once been a magnificent garden was now a tangled collection of tall grass, thorny weeds, and downed branches.

"*Little* project?" replied Will, a **bemused** smile on his lips.

Dr. Perez grinned, "Yes, I suppose it's not so little. Can you tackle it?"

Will nodded **ardently**. A job this large could put him through college. And it would mean he'd see Laura every day. With that, they said their good-byes.

Will arrived home to the **noxious** smell of Ken's latest effort: curried avocado casserole. In order to protect himself from this latest creation, Will downed some bread before taking his place at the table. Maybe the **viscous** brown gravy would help smother the taste. Staring down at the concoction, steeling himself to consume it, Will took a deep breath and slid a forkful into his mouth. It wasn't nearly as bad as he'd imagined, but it certainly wasn't good. The Indian spices didn't **complement** the avocado's flavor, and the overall **fusion** of ingredients and **cuisines** didn't sit well in his stomach.

"Tastes like chicken," he muttered, hoping he could stop at that. Thankfully, his parents changed the topic.

"Have you met the new neighbors yet?"

"Yeah," Will answered and then put his fork down, for good. "I ran into the girl who moved in there. She seems nice."

When Joanne heard the words *girl* and *nice*, her ears perked up, and she leaned forward, elbows on the table. "So, what's her name?"

"Laura." Will **feigned** a casual air. "Laura Perez, I think. Her father's a historian. They've moved around a lot."

Joanne pressed on. "What about her mother?"

"Dead. Cancer." As Will uttered the words, they **resonated** deep within him. He imagined the **void** Laura must have felt losing a parent like that. It was beyond horrible.

Joanne **concurred** with Will's unspoken thought. "Oh, that poor thing." She looked in Stone Manor's direction, though it could hardly be seen through the wall.

"Yeah. She told me that when we were walking around town. I kind of gave her the grand tour."

"Well, I'm glad to see that you reached out to her." Joanne sat back at last. "I'm proud of you, Will." With that, she spooned some more casserole onto his plate and turned to Ken. "We should really go over there tomorrow and introduce ourselves."

Ken nodded **emphatically**, and with his eyebrows raised in inspiration, offered, "I'll bake a pie."

Will shot a glance at his mother and she silently mouthed back, "Don't worry. I'll help him."

The trio stared at their barely eaten plates. At this point, the gravy was beginning to **coagulate**. But rather than melt it in the microwave and serve more, Ken collected the dishes and lifted the phone. Turning to his family, "Sausage or pepperoni?" *He's beginning to catch on,* thought Will.

* * *

Laura was standing at the end of a hallway. At first, it looked like she was dancing with someone, but as Will drew closer, he realized that she was fighting, struggling desperately against the powerful and elephantine shadow creature.

Will ran to save her. The corridor around him began to twist, knocking him off-balance, and **thwarted** his attempt to rescue her. He punched the walls in frustration, and they **undulated**, but he presssed on.

At long last, Will reached the end of the hallway. But then, just as he got to Laura, the darkness **enshrouded** her, and she was gone.

CHAPTER SIX

Between midnight and 6:00 A.M., the lone traffic light in town was set to pulse yellow. At 6:01 A.M., it began its normal daytime cycle, from red to green to yellow.

Most townsfolk weren't even aware of the late-night shift in pattern. So when the light began furiously flashing yellow just before noon, traffic in Red Fork was thrown into gridlock. Cars screeched to a halt, and drivers craned their necks out their windows to see what caused the disruption. Their curiosity was quickly—and disastrously—satisfied. Seconds after the light flickered its **portent**, a deafening explosion shook the business district.

Pedestrians out on their lunch break fell to the pavement, and car doors slammed shut as drivers ran to their rescue. In the sunlight, a plume of smoke rose **ominously** and steadily from Sal's Pizzeria. Heads turned as patrons stumbled out of the brick building, their faces covered in soot. Two construction workers nearby grabbed their hardhats and rushed past the coughing victims into the dark entry to rescue others still trapped inside. The distant wail of a siren grew louder, and drivers rushed to move their cars and make room for the fire trucks speeding toward the **conflagration**.

A crowd gathered slowly on the sidewalk outside the pizzeria, Will and Ty among them. Keeping a safe distance, they stared dumbfounded at the blackened doorframe and waited with bated breath for any signs of life. Sal's wife pushed through the mob, screaming hysterically, "Sal! Sal! Where are you?" She would have run headlong into the smoking building had it not been for the sheriff, who arrived in time to pull her back. Freeing herself from his restraining arms, Marie collapsed to the ground, her body convulsing with sobs. "No," she moaned, her hands reaching up to cover her grief-stricken face. "No, please no...." Friends knelt beside her with comforting arms.

Behind the onlookers, firefighters hopped down from their truck and aimed their water hoses at the blaze, moving quickly to extinguish the flames. One **intrepid** fireman stormed the building, disappearing into the billowing smoke with **abandon**. Meanwhile, the sheriff hastily cordoned off the surrounding block, directing the concerned crowd behind the police barricades.

As they watched the inferno slowly **dissipate**, Will glanced at his fellow bystanders, reading in their expressions the same shock and worry that reverberated in his own. Tense moments passed before the firefighters conclusively doused the fire. The **plucky** fireman who had run into the pizzeria emerged unscathed, supporting an overcome Sal, and was followed by the two courageous hardhats.

The sight of Sal bathed in black soot, his apron stained a bright red hue, **elicited** a collective gasp from the crowd. Marie shrieked and began swooning, her face pale from weeping. Sal looked down at his spattered cooking smock, swiped his thumb across it, and much to everyone's surprise, stuck the digit into his mouth.

"Marinara sauce," he explained, smacking his lips, "The best I ever made." He looked back at his smoking restaurant and shook his head. "Damn shame."

Everyone sighed in relief, a few people even chuckling at Sal's astoundingly blasé quip. Marie rushed to her husband and clutched him, her tender words of gratitude muffled by his shoulder. Presently, she pulled back and faced him squarely, her eyes **glowering**. "Don't you *ever* scare me like that again!" With that, she kissed him passionately, pulled his arm around her shoulder, and with the sheriff's assistance, guided him to a waiting ambulance.

Harrumphing to get the audience's attention, the fire chief informed them that the blaze had started in the kitchen. "The gas line must have leaked and caught fire. We were able to contain it to the kitchen, and fortunately there's no structural damage." His **terse** report over, he strode back to the fire engine, neglecting to address the smoke that flooded the dining area.

As curious onlookers always do, the crowd ventured in for a closer look at the destruction. Sal emerged from the ambulance, his smock replaced by a clean shirt. "It's gonna take a lot of paint," he **lamented**, examining the blackened-out window frames. "I was in the vestibule between the kitchen and the counter when all of a sudden there's this big—" he gestured wildly with his arms, "This gigantic rumble under my feet, and then the whole place started shaking. Everything started falling off the shelves—olive oil all over the floor." He dropped his head into his hands. "I thought it was an earthquake. I thought, 'This is it, Sal. You're dead.'" He thumped his chest. "Then the oven blew up. The door came flying right at me—woosh!—but somehow I ducked behind the corner. Must have hit my head on something, 'cause that's all I remember until I was out here."

No sooner had he described the event than another loud crash came from inside the pizzeria. The crowd jumped back in fear.

Firefighters **loitering** near their truck cautiously stepped back into the pizzeria and soon announced their findings. The small wall separating the kitchen from the vestibule collapsed. "Don't worry," offered the fire chief to a **morose** Sal, "that's not a load-bearing wall."

Sal didn't care whether or not the wall was **superfluous** to the overall structure of the building. To him, its very existence was **integral**, for it was the only thing that had protected him from the oven door as it hurled toward him.

On further investigation, the collapsed partition led to another discovery. Inside the wall in a hollowed-out space, a stash of old liquor bottles was found. Based on their shape and the amount of dust that had gathered, they had probably been there since the 1920s, which made them the product of the illegal bootlegging **industry**. That, Will remembered, had been made famous in Red Fork by one Johnny Gunn.

* * *

After an **unheralded** rise through the ranks of organized crime in the Prohibition Era, Johnny Gunn made a name for himself by brewing and smuggling alcoholic beverages. His clientele ranged from elderly widows living off their husbands' meager pensions to members of the wealthy elite. Some of his customers wanted "a little nip" for their coffees, while others bought cases of the "hooch" for their **clandestine** speakeasies and other **illicit** establishments.

Regarded as an impresario, Gunn often threw lavish parties. At any one of these spectacles, one could expect to rub elbows with European royalty or the American equivalent. In fact, according to one well-documented affair, Gunn climbed on top of a table and sang for his **inebriated** partygoers, while Babe Ruth provided an unlikely accompaniment on the piano.

Johnny Gunn's magnetic personality had translated into huge demand for his liquor, and in no time at all, he was rich beyond his wildest dreams. New-found millions in hand, he then sought to conquer the business world—investing in the stock market, taking up golf, and marrying an heiress. Pure **avarice** had helped transform Gunn from a common hoodlum to a refined gentleman. After buying his way into high society, all that was missing was an equally regal home—and that turned out to be Stone Manor.

Arriving in Red Fork in 1925, Gunn was the first person to live in the mansion since McAllister had died. Town residents were guarded. But since Gunn's new neighbors had been McAllister's own servants, most were pleased to see Stone Manor reoccupied—even if by someone with such **notoriety**. Still, Gunn wanted to **assuage** any doubts over his checkered past, so he **bestowed** a generous sum of money to the building of a statue—a statue of McAllister. That tribute now stood in the park.

But, as the **adage** goes, old habits die hard. Gunn moved not only his wife and their personal property to Red Fork, but also his bootlegging operation. Before long, he was once again hosting parties with an **ample** supply of liquor. No one knew where he was producing the alcohol or how he transported the **copious** supply to cities like Pittsburgh and Cleveland, but people **hypothesized** that he discreetly shipped it up the river on a barge, all right under the noses of the local authorities. Either that, or they simply looked the other way in exchange for a monthly **gratuity**.

In his first year as a resident, Johnny Gunn's profession remained the same, though his personality began to change. The man who was once "everybody's friend" became unpredictable and visibly **irascible**. At another well-attended party in the fall of 1926, Gunn went from delightful host to out-of-control monster in the blink of an eye when he shoved a man to the floor and then socked out his eye. An **indignant** Gunn justified his action, saying, "The guy was looking at my wife. Nobody looks at her except me." That night had been the turning point: After that, there would be no more social gatherings at Stone Manor.

Other strange stories began to emerge from the mansion. Gunn installed his own movie projector so he could watch Tom Mix western serials every night. He nailed the windows shut and changed the locks routinely, fearing bandits would invade his home and steal his fortune. He stopped eating at some point, subsisting on only his **potent** bathtub gin. And, he claimed to hear a disembodied voice chanting the name "Melvin."

This final experience proved especially disquieting to Gunn. Johnny Gunn had not been his true name. Having the misfortune to be born Melvin Krakowsky in Peoria, Illinois, his new name suggested the type of person he envisioned himself to be.

Unfortunately, the **alias** was **ironic** to say the least. Poor Melvin was so near-sighted that he wouldn't have been able to shoot the side of a blimp from 50 yards away. Ultimately, his **myopic** condition, coupled with his famous **pseudonym** and his growing paranoia, led to his demise.

Venturing to the outskirts of town one evening, Gunn went to meet some potential investors. They offered him money and also protection from rival gangsters and "desperados." The problem was, his "new clients" were in fact FBI agents, seeking out his criminal activities. Gunn's **erratic** behavior had clouded his once **keen** judgment.

After a brief melee, Gunn managed to escape. The G-men chased him down McAllister Boulevard. When Gunn took a corner too sharply, his car flipped, and he managed to get out and duck behind a tire. As per his custom, he had armed himself with a loaded Colt .45—his "six-shooter"—but Gunn had never fired the weapon until this fateful night. He shot first, aiming straight at the agent in front of him, but missed his mark by a wide margin. The agent returned fire with better precision, and was followed in short **succession** by his equally skilled comrades. Melvin Krakowsky fell dead in a **volley** of bullets.

Gunn's distillery was located later, when the police searched Stone Manor, along with **shards** from broken bottles and the painted mannequin. But the vast supply of alcohol that he had intended to sell was never found. That is, until now. Apparently,

Gunn had hidden his illegal inventory in the coal storage bins that were now in Sal's Pizzeria.

*   *   *

With the flames out and Sal seemingly free of any lasting injury, the relieved crowd **dispersed** from the scene. Will and Ty headed toward the park, escaping the **fetid** smell, though the incident loomed large in their conversation.

"If I'd been working today," Ty realized, his mouth shaping the words before he could even form them in his mind, "I would have been right there. Right next door. It really makes you think." He gazed up, taking in the blue sky and soft white clouds with a renewed sense of awe.

"Yeah, it's weird. We were just there the other day." Although the fire also shocked him, Will downplayed it to **mollify** his apprehensive friend. "But it doesn't look that bad. Like Sal said—just a few coats of paint and it'll be like old times. And the video store wasn't damaged at all." Glancing at Ty, Will looked for signs that his words had **placated** his friend.

"You're right," Ty's intense expression softened into his trademark grin. "Sal must have really burned the calzones today!" Ty stunned himself as much as Will by his **capricious** remark, and they both doubled over laughing. Barely making it to a bench, they collapsed in **mirth**. Given the anxiety they'd just experienced, this release was more than welcome.

Their conversation soon turned quiet. For the first time in quite a while, Will felt bonded to his oldest friend, and it seemed the right time to **broach** some things. "So, where are you thinking of applying to?"

Ty pointed east, in the direction of McAllister College. "What do you think?" he asked. From his tone, Will could tell he actually meant, "Where else would I go?" Ty sighed loudly, his tone filled with **ennui**. "Hey, it makes the most sense."

Will thought quite the opposite. *Going there makes the least sense.* He wanted to challenge Ty about his logic, but instead held his tongue. He didn't want to **quell** the lighthearted mood, so he changed the subject to something more **innocuous**. "I didn't know you were working at the antique store."

Ty fidgeted in his seat. "Oh, no … I'm not working there," he answered, avoiding Will's gaze. "I was just helping out for a few days. No biggie." He rubbed the back of his neck and then **scrutinized** the grime that had accumulated on his hand. "Geez. I'm sweating up a storm out here. I've got to find me some A/C." He finally looked at Will.

Will could see that Ty was uneasy, holding back. *Why do I keep pushing it?* Will **chastised** himself, angry that he'd brought up college in the first place. He knew it was a **divisive** issue, both at home and with his friends; it only separated him from others, like so many things he did.

The silence was mounting between them, and Will was **wary** of pressing the topic. To bring in some **levity**, he chose instead to confirm tomorrow's plans. "Are we still on for sailing? Laura's psyched." Then, almost as an afterthought, "And so am I."

"Sure." Ty smiled **feebly**. "Should be great."

The wind around them shifted, causing the smell of burnt air to waft over them. Ty pinched his nose and looked at Will. This time, their silence was mutually understood: It was time to go. Ty turned to jog toward the antique store, and Will headed for home. "See ya later!"

"Stay safe," Ty called back in a nasal voice. Letting go of his nose, he repeated the warning again, this time in his usual baritone, and disappeared around a corner.

Will crossed the street, only to feel the soft asphalt through his sneakers. It was buckling in the extreme summer heat. He wanted to get home and inside as quickly as possible, but the faster he went, the more uncomfortable he felt. Finally, he had to stop, seeking shelter under one of the **expansive** oak trees along the street.

Stretching out the neck of his tee-shirt seemed liked the next good idea. Will blew down onto his chest to cool himself, and as various people passed by, he smiled in response to the occasional **salutation**.

"Hot enough for ya?"

"Could hit 100 today."

Nod, smile, wave of the hand.

Outside the Historical Society down the block, Daniel Bell was chatting with Dr. Perez. They seemed quite **engaged** in conversation, at times even laughing. It struck Will that Perez seemed very interested in whatever Bell was telling him—in fact, it amused him. He recalled Bell's annual visits to the school: an event worthy of a special student assembly. Everyone would crowd into the gym (which doubled as auditorium and cafeteria), and Bell would **drone** on about a phase of McAllister's life in **excruciating** detail. Year in, year out, it was always the same phase. Ty couldn't help but dub the **keynote** address "Snoozapalooza."

By what Will could tell from across the road, Bell had not **abridged** his lecture at all, even for an audience of one. The two men moved inside the old gatehouse and Will, sufficiently cooled by his **respite** in the shade, continued on his way. Walking slowly, he arrived back at his house, where he immediately set up camp in front of the living room's air conditioner.

Hours later, after the crisp air had cooled Will to a comfortable level, he sat with his parents for dinner. Tonight, Ken's culinary brainchild was gazpacho. The cold soup was an excellent choice for such a balmy day, but Ken's **prowess** with the menu selection proved far more refined than his actual preparation of the dish.

Will slurped the gazpacho loudly, in hopes that the unappealing sound would suffice for his comment on the meal.

His parents eyed him curiously though remained silent. He bit into his mother's normally scrumptious homemade cornbread, but today it tasted like cardboard. His father's cooking had managed to dull his **gustatory** senses.

"Did you hear about Sal's?" Joanne asked, as she poured Will a glass of water. "I'm just relieved no one got hurt. Dr. Perez told us this morning when we stopped by for a visit."

"Dr. Perez?" *How did Perez know about the fire? It occurred before he'd even been down to talk to Bell.*

"He's quite a character," Ken offered sarcastically. "He reminds me of Jonny Quest's father." Will's quizzical expression prompted him to explain. "You know, from the cartoon."

"Quest is right," Joanne chimed in. "The good doctor has been all over the world, and he's dragged that poor daughter of his along with him. She's probably never even had a real home—at least not for very long." Joanne looked pointedly at Will. "I'd like you to really make an effort to get to know her." She grabbed his hand to **beseech** him further. "I'm sure she could use a friend."

At a loss for words, Will blushed his signature crimson.

"I don't think you need to twist his arm!" Ken **retorted** with a smirk.

CHAPTER SEVEN

The next morning, Will was up and out early. Four lawns were on his roster, and he wanted to get them done so he could go sailing with his friends. He also wanted to be finished before the sun reached its **zenith**. It had rained overnight, but the water had already evaporated in the ever-worsening heat. His first customer of the day, Mrs. O'Leary, was outside when he arrived at her plain **quadrilateral** of a yard.

In the summer, O'Leary became a different person. Freed from the shackles of her **authoritarian** teaching role, she was now warm and pleasant. "Morning, Will. What'll it be this week? A Matisse? Picasso?" She was one of the few clients who appreciated his personal style of lawn care.

"Not sure. I'm thinking of experimenting today. A stream of consciousness thing. Do you mind?"

"Go right ahead. After all," she said, winking, "If it doesn't turn out right, I know it'll always grow back." With that, she handed him an envelope containing his money—she was also one of the only people to pay him in advance. To Will, this was a warm gesture, one that signified confidence in his ability.

Will set his mower at the intersection of the driveway and the sidewalk, and pulled the engine cord. The gas-powered brush took off and the machine moved easily along the edge of the lawn. Will let his mind wander, hoping his thoughts would lead to an original portrait.

Naturally, the first image he **conjured** was Mrs. O'Leary. Free association often led people to recall recent events, Will knew. In this case, his teacher was back in class for that last math test, which Will ended up passing with high marks.

Mrs. O'Leary had just collected the test booklets, and Will was feeling both dread and excitement—dread because he hadn't been prepared for the **arduous** exam, and excitement because summer was finally here. But in that fleeting moment, he had also felt a rush—about the infinite possibilities of his life, **pristine** and uncorrupted. Maneuvering the mower to his left, Will curved a line in the grass. The line soon became an arc, and the arc, a figure.

Will thought about when he first met Laura: her **lithe** form and the colorful **montage** she'd provided about the places she'd been.

A picturesque Spanish landscape came to mind, and suddenly, he and Laura were there! From high atop a Moor castle, the two gazed down on the Mediterranean Sea. The **granular** stone walls were **palpable** against his fingers, and Will could almost taste the salty air. Soon, they were in Paris, with the Eiffel Tower majestically behind them. They strolled along the River Seine arm-in-arm.

Will snapped back to reality. The mower's blade was scraping against the curb. *No, I'm not ready to leave yet.* He freed the mower and then closed his eyes, returning to Laura and the City of Lights. She smiled at him, and Will realized from her gaze that he had changed. No longer the shy Will Lassiter with a **predisposition** for passivity, he was an **aberration** of himself, now **audacious** and unpredictable.

"This is wonderful, but a bit **pedestrian**...." With that, Will and Laura found themselves in a raft on the Colorado River, navigating around rocks and other **protrusions**. "I can't believe you talked me into this!" Laura shouted as she clung to a rope.

Will, on the other hand, was invigorated. They paddled through the rough water, narrowly avoiding several boulders, taking in the reddish-brown warmth of the **ravine**. There was no place like this in Red Fork. Water sprayed up over the bow of the raft, dousing Will and Laura.

When he regained his **acuity**, they were standing in an airplane 3,000 feet high. They stepped toward the opening.

"Geronimo!"

Will leapt out of the airplane with **abandon**, spiraling through the air. Laura screamed in glee as they fell. Pulling their ripcords, they drifted peacefully before landing in a carpet of plush grass. Will rolled onto his knees and stood up: Laura was gone, along with the parachute and Paris and the canyon. He was back on O'Leary's property.

His heart still pounding from his daydream, Will was happily **mused**. He applied the finishing touches to his grassy artwork. There, on his math teacher's lawn, he had fashioned an unmistakable likeness—of himself.

All this daydreaming put Will in a nostalgic mood. He thought back to his childhood, to when he'd lost so many friends. His friendship with Ty was the most upsetting. Will jerked the mower to the right, then back to the left. *What happened to us?* There was no open **animosity**, but they were clearly parting ways. Was this friendship to suffer the same fate as all the others?

Will grew anxious, trying desperately to uncover his **foibles**. He had to do something to help salvage his friendship with Ty.

Will's search was **futile**. He couldn't think of anything he had done wrong. Maybe Brady was right—maybe he was just a "freak." *Ty has humored me long enough. I'm just slowing him down, and he knows it.*

Will swung the mower around for a final pass, and his mind drifted to dinner the previous night. His father had made an

incriminating remark that left Will blushing, though his mother diplomatically changed the subject.

"I heard some strange noises coming from your room last night. Is everything all right?"

"Just a bad dream." Will fell silent, wondering whether to clarify his statement. "Actually, I've been having a lot of nightmares lately."

"Oh?" Ken tilted up his head, waiting for details.

"It's hard to describe. I'm in Stone Manor, and there are these stairs that keep ... going down...." He struggled to find the words, to paint the scene so they could visualize it. "And the walls keep moving.... There's a woman and she's screaming." He paused to see if his parents were listening.

They were. Ken and Joanne exchanged puzzled glances, and Joanne opened her mouth. "That's rather disturbing."

Will was annoyed at his mother's statement of the obvious. "Yeah, I know!"

Ken tried to reassure his son that these were just dreams, but Will wasn't convinced. "I'd get nightmares too if I watched as many horror movies and ate as much junk food as you do," Joanne **admonished**, shooting over a disapproving glance.

Horror movies? Junk food? You've got to be kidding. Will wanted to tell them about the dark figure that **skulked** around in his dream, but they'd probably think it was his **fecund** imagination.

"Have a warm glass of milk before you go to sleep tonight."

Will's **agitation** only increased. Clearly, his parents weren't taking him seriously. They could offer only pat solutions involving less television and more warm milk. He was totally alone.

A **morose** Will **sullenly** shut off the mower. Made **abject** by his meandering thoughts, he started off for his next job, not bothering to look back at the self-portrait he had carved. If he had, he would have seen a jagged line slashed across his face—a jagged line just like the scar on his arm.

CHAPTER EIGHT

Finally, it was time to go sailing—with Laura. Will quickly showered and went to meet her in front of Stone Manor.

As usual, Laura looked stunning. She had on a black one-piece bathing suit and a semi-sheer wrap, topped by an oversized hat. With some **trepidation**, Will told her she looked great. He was reminded of how stylish she had looked in his daydream. They set off and, chattering away, barely noticed when they'd arrived at the lake.

Over a mile long, Red Fork Lake was ideal for sailing, fishing, and other **aquatic** sports. In the winter, it froze over, perfect for skating, and throughout the year, it provided **potable** water. The lake had earned its Red Fork name because, like a fork, it split on one edge, creating two slender channels alongside the main body. As for the "red," that was because each year, red clay deposits from the terrain above would trickle down to the shore, temporarily turning the water crimson.

Will and Laura arrived at the boathouse. Another remnant of McAllister's estate, it looked like a large barn, doors opening directly onto the lake. McAllister had been an accomplished rower in his university days, and he used the boathouse to store his **sundry** boats. The annual "by invitation only" boat race was held here—no doubt to accommodate McAllister's wealthy friends. In one well-publicized match, he had defeated Cornelius Vanderbilt by more than 20 lengths.

The boathouse went to Johnny Gunn when he purchased the mansion, as it had been listed on Stone Manor's deed. Gunn wasted no time in replacing McAllister's small boats with a barge he used to ferry his liquor. More recently, the townspeople bought the building, thinking it would make a much-needed rec center.

The investment paid off. Today, it was a necessary gateway for anyone interested in, well, water. For a small fee, one could rent sailboats, kayaks, and paddleboats. To boot, all kids in town were entitled to swimming lessons there **gratis**.

On the adjoining boardwalk, Will spotted Ty and Katie near the snack bar. *I'll just play it cool and let him set the tone.* Will **resolved** to steer clear of any controversies with his friend today.

"I got us a couple of sailfish," Ty said, as he pointed to two small boats moored to the bulkhead. "Everything else was already gone, so I grabbed what I could."

Will followed Ty onto one of the boats, while Katie and Laura boarded the other. They paddled away from the roped-off swimming area so as to hoist the sails. No sooner had they done that than a steady breeze cropped up, carrying them to the center of the lake. Clearly, this wasn't going to be a **placid** ride. Ty steered the boat, while Will, a sailing **novice**, followed his orders to hold the rope taut. An **analogous** situation was unfolding on the other boat, where Laura trusted Katie's directions.

Picking up speed, the boat began to lift out of the water. Ty was trying to catch as much wind as possible, which put them at risk to tip over. Having no desire to flip, Will leaned against the side of the boat to **countervail** the strong gust and successfully settled it down into the water again. He looked over at Ty and was met with a disapproving shake of the head. He knew that Ty enjoyed recreating **maritime** disasters, but friends or not, he preferred to stay dry.

Katie and Laura's boat had fallen behind. Will waved back, while Ty shouted, "Get goin', ladies—losers buy lunch!"

Inspired by the wager, Laura let out the sail, flying them past a **bemused** Will and an **indignant** Ty. Not one to be outdone, Will released his sail, and with Ty tacking the boat in the same path, they navigated the wake to catch up to the girls. His expertise at hand, Ty pulled into the lead for good.

The finish line awaited them at the entrance to the cove. Will lowered the sail to slow, while they watched their frustrated

antagonists catch up. Ty started to utter a wisecrack, but Katie cut him off first. "Shut … up," she **exhorted** through clenched teeth. Will and Ty high-fived in response and then **tethered** the two crafts together. Now confident that his friendship with Ty was intact, Will anchored the boats to halt their movement.

"That was fun!" Laura exclaimed, using the mast to steady herself as she stood up. Not one to **procrastinate**, she tossed her hat onto the seat and dove gracefully into the water. With a series of **deft** strokes, she swam away from the bobbing boats, gliding across the surface of the lake. She was a **proficient** swimmer, Will could see, her stroke powerful and fast.

The three others quickly followed. The sharp cold was a much needed break from the baking sun. With soft clay cushioning their toes, Will and Ty began splashing each other, while Katie and Laura rolled their eyes.

"What's that?" Laura asked, pointing to a mound built up in the red silt.

Will looked down through the **limpid** water, his hair dripping. "It's a zebra mussel." He bent over to **dislodge** it and showed it to her. Just one of the many freshwater **mollusks** in Red Fork Lake, the mussel's name came from the white and black stripes that adorned its shell.

As he knelt to put the mussel back, Will was struck by something on Laura's right leg: a long, raised cut stretched from her ankle to the middle of her calf. From its reddish complexion, it looked like a recent injury, perhaps as recent as the last day or so. *Another fall down the stairs?* he wondered, remembering the bruise on her forehead. But before he could ask, Laura plunged into the water, her leg disappearing beneath the surface. Will turned pink at the thought that she'd caught him looking at her legs. He wanted to ask her about it but decided to keep mum for now.

The **quaternary** of friends swam back to their boats and lounged on the decks. A swan and her **cygnet** paddled by and honked. Unlike his graceful mother, the baby swan struggled against the current, ruffling his gray feathers. "When they're young, they look like that," Will explained to Laura. "He'll turn white when he's older."

"You guys are so lucky," said Laura. "It's so peaceful here. What a great place to grow up." She rolled onto her stomach and admired the **pacific** scene, waves **lapping** against the boat.

Will couldn't help but glance at Laura over and over again, though he tried not to be obvious. Lounging on the sailfish, her tanned skin dotted with water, she glowed as she worked her fingers through her long, damp hair. She looked content, which made her all the more appealing.

"I met your father the other day," Katie chirped, interrupting Will's thought. She was addressing Laura. "He came to my parents' store to drop off some things he'd found at the manor. He told us you guys went scuba diving off the Great Barrier Reef." With **adulation** in her voice, "He is *so* cool!"

"Thanks," Laura replied **sheepishly**. "I guess he is, though it's kind of hard to think of your own dad as being cool."

"Your dad *totally* is," Katie enthused, sitting up. "Mine, on the other hand, well, let's just say his favorite hobby is collecting coins."

"**Numismatics?**" Laura excitedly blurted out. Then, turning a fiery shade of red, "I think that's what it's called." But she couldn't hide her enthusiasm.

"Oh my God, you too?" Katie's jaw dropped, her voice echoing through the cove. "I would never have guessed—"

"That I'm a coin geek?" Laura's lips curled into a distorted grin, but she spoke with assurance. "Guilty as charged."

"I had a stamp collection when I was a kid," Ty piped in.

Katie blushed at her turn, "And I still have my Barbie dolls."

The four teens shared a hearty laugh, and as Will snickered, he was overcome by a sense of relief. Ty and Katie were treating Laura like one of their own, and she was clearly warmed by that. But even more so, Will was struck by her **disclosure**. She was becoming real to him and **attainable**—not some glorified fantasy, but a human being with quirks. *Just like me,* he thought.

Not one of the foursome noticed a sailboat approach until it had **occluded** the sunlight. At once in the shade, the friends found themselves face to face with Ty's brother.

Three years older than Ty, Ray Martin was a larger, more impressive version of his younger brother. His faded McAllister High T-shirt clung to his muscular chest, and his dark chocolate complexion, several notches deeper than Ty's, displayed his passion for outdoor activities. "Hey guys," he **bellowed** in greeting, and nodding at Laura, "You must be the girl from Stone Manor."

"Yup, that's me. How's it going?" Laura waved back.

Ray took off his sunglasses and slung them on his collar. "So, did my little brother tell you he was going to beat me today?" His eyes remained on Laura, but he was clearly talking to Ty.

"No ... in fact," Laura boldly continued, "I didn't even know Ty had a brother. He's never mentioned you."

Will and Ty doubled over in laughter, **chortling** noisily at Laura's reply. Her **flippant** tone struck a nerve with Ray, too, but he **feigned** indifference.

"That doesn't surprise me," he shouted, loud enough to be heard over his brother's **mirth**. "I wouldn't want to mention it if some guy kept kicking my—"

"What is it that you want?" Katie hollered over the **cacophony** of voices. She'd seen this too many times—Ray aggravating Ty until they duked it out in one sport or another.

The result was always the same: Ray would win. In fact, Ray knew he would win and he was **smug** about it. Ignoring Katie, he called back, "You know—a race. How about it, bro? Or are you scared?" He cupped his hands to his mouth and loudly mocked his younger sibling, "Bock! Bock! Bock!"

This **gibe** didn't result in the outburst Ray was hoping for. In fact, Ty barely responded. Instead, he calmly set about collecting some excess rope, and spooled it around the mast. His **stoic** response **infuriated** Ray.

"What's the matter, Ty? Don't want to be embarrassed in front of your friends?" He shook his head, "Every morning you tell me how you're gonna win, but now when the race is finally here, you're quiet? Sheesh...." He **grimaced** and stormed off into his boat, though he made sure to remain within earshot.

Ty felt he had to **acquiesce**. "Okay, then, let's finish this."

A **coup**. Ray had finally managed to get his brother to race, and he wasted no time maneuvering his boat alongside Ty's. After Will hopped into the girls' boat, they were ready, and with a count to three, the sails were off. A **hardy** gust of wind pushed them quickly to the middle of the lake.

Ray took the early lead, but Ty followed close behind. In just a few short minutes, they had spanned the diameter of the lake, and were fast approaching the mouth of the river. In front, a buoy floated, warning of the shallow water near the **delta**. Whoever sailed around the buoy and back to the cove first, won.

As they headed into the turn, Ty moved his rudder to get on the inside track. His plan was to cut around Ray at the buoy and take the lead in the final stretch. But just as he neared Ray's boat, his brother swerved in front, **stymieing** his move. As a result, Ty turned too close to the buoy, and couldn't right the boat immediately. He pulled hard on the rudder, hoping to keep from steering far off course. But by turning the boat so hard, he **deleteriously** knocked it off-balance. Ty flipped into the lake.

Scissor-kicking to the surface, Ty watched as Ray took the turn cleanly. Shifting his sail to the boat's other side, Ray picked up momentum. As he headed for the finish line, Ty floated in his wake, reminded once again of his older brother's superiority and nautical **prowess**.

Will, Laura, and Katie watched Ty's mishap from the cove and quickly sailed toward him. After his friends helped him right the overturned sailfish, Ty gloomily **assessed** the damage. Aside from the soaked sail and ropes, there was a small leak near the stern, and a tiny crack in the rudder's inner. The boat was taking on water from this **breach**.

"It'll need to be **caulked**, but I think I can sail her in," Ty said, dejected. "But the back needs to be out of the water. Will, can you sit at the front as a counterweight?"

Within minutes, they were all back on shore. As they returned the boat to an attendant, Katie sidled over to Ty and patted him gently. "You almost had him this time."

"I suppose," Ty grinned, appreciative of her attempt to **console** him, "but I seem to remember that there was another race today— one in which the losers were supposed to buy us lunch?" With that, they meandered to the the snack bar and then onto the beach. Their hot dogs were gone in seconds.

Today, as most summer days, scores of blankets and umbrellas littered the coastline. The lake was a popular retreat. Will stretched out on his towel, closing his eyes. He listened to the **myriad** sounds around him: the hum of an airplane, the crunch of feet against sand, the **sonorous** laughter of children **cavorting** in the water. But just when he was beginning to doze, his **serenity** was shattered. He heard a familiar voice.

"Hi, I'm Brady."

Will opened his eyes and cringed. Brady stood over Laura, his well-tanned body **casting** a shadow across Will.

"I'm Laura," she smiled, squinting up.

Brady tucked his unruly blond hair under his baseball cap. "I heard you moved into the old McAllister place."

Will was **livid**. Brady was handsome, athletic, and **affable**, and he spoke with an insincerity that seemed to fool everyone—from teachers to parents to his teenage **peers**. He was popular, to say the least, particularly with girls, and though he was dating someone, he was always on the make. Poor Jasmine was aware of her boyfriend's two-timing ways; she'd even caught him red-handed once. But for some **inextricable** reason, she always took him back. Brady was able to get away with this behavior because few people realized just how **unctuous** he was. Will was in this small minority. He wanted to warn Laura, but there was no opportunity to do so.

"Hey, we should get together," Brady crooned in his **suave** tone, "I'd love to show you around."

"That sounds nice," Laura replied in a friendly manner.

"Are you doing anything tomorrow?"

Will watched in silent horror as the two hammered out details for their date. He rolled onto his other side to escape the depressing scene and spotted Jasmine under a nearby umbrella. She was staring at them, seething with jealousy. *At least I'm not the only one,* Will thought. Jasmine rose abruptly and stormed off the beach.

Another hour went by, and Will was still waiting for the right moment to pull Laura aside. Brady had stationed himself right next to her, though, so there was no chance to break in. And when Will rose to leave, Laura wanted to stay longer, making him feel even more rejected. *That was fast. She's been here a week, and already she's dumping me for someone more normal.*

By the time he'd reached his house, Will's back was stinging with pain. Beet red from sunburn, he'd forgotten to apply sunscreen. Now he'd be in agony all night.

Adding insult to injury, his mother spoke up. "Oh Will, I forgot to tell you, we saw Ty and Katie the other night." She spooned some creamed spinach onto his plate. "They were at the movies together. Holding hands."

"I think they make a cute couple," Joanne continued, and then, looking up from her pork chops, "So, how are things between you and Laura?"

As soon as he could escape the dinner table, Will crashed in his room. *Ty and Katie?* He was shocked. But after a few minutes of consideration, he grudgingly admitted, *Yeah, I suppose I can see it. But why didn't I see it coming?* Annoyed by his blindness, Will searched his brain to remember clues: Ty's **evasiveness** when Will asked him about working at the antique store, and the fact that Ty and Katie just happened to be busy at the same times. It all made sense. Will's mood grew grim. Obviously, they were hiding their relationship from him, and judging by their behavior, wanted more time for themselves. Which meant less time with him.

He glanced out his window at Stone Manor. Laura was probably home by now. *I don't want to bother her the night before her big date,* he thought sarcastically. A wave of loneliness, mingled with resentment and jealousy, came over him. **Despondent**, he reached over and pulled down the shades.

*   *   *

The frayed white curtains billowed out as Will passed by them, and the incoming breeze chilled his **ashen** skin. He was in a long hallway, dark but for the moonlight filtering in through the **translucent** drapes. Putting his hand to the mahogany wall, he knew instantly he was in Stone Manor.

The wind **subsided**, and he could hear a woman's voice pleading, "No! Please, no!"

Will headed toward the **plaintive** pleas, up the stairs and around corners. He followed the **sinuous** corridor in search of the imperiled woman. The pleading was nonstop, though it was soon extinguished by an infant's crying wails. It all seemed familiar to Will, as in that **labyrinth** of his youth, when he wandered the manor's halls for the exit.

The crying grew louder, and Will began to sprint. Reaching a doorway, he was blocked by a man's threatening shape, and though his glistening black eyes were all Will could see, the **malevolent** presence was enough to terrify him.

Will took a step back from the **impasse**, but something grabbed his arm. He struggled, but the grip only tightened....

* * *

Will woke up in a sweat, his arm tangled in his blanket. He tugged at it in **exasperation** and, finally freeing himself, threw it on the floor angrily. *These nightmares are really starting to tick me off.* He flipped over and felt the stinging throb of sunburn on his back. He groaned in frustration.

CHAPTER NINE

Will looked at his appointment calendar, and his heart sank. He had only one job today, but it was to clean up the property around Stone Manor for Dr. Perez. That meant Laura would be there. Will wasn't sure what, if anything, he'd say to her about Brady—he didn't want to come off sounding jealous and resentful. With a heavy sigh, he collected his tools, piled them in a wheelbarrow, and trudged next door.

Will was relieved to see Dr. Perez outside already, busy scraping paint off an old armoire. It saved him from having to knock on the door and risk meeting Laura face-to-face. They exchanged pleasantries for a moment before Dr. Perez resumed scraping. Conscious that Will was studying him, he straightened up.

"I'm trying to strip off the paint," he explained. "For some reason, back in the forties and fifties, people covered up beautiful wood with gobs of paint. This one," he gestured at the wardrobe, "has at least four layers, and in the gaudiest colors you can imagine. I'm hoping I can restore it to its natural condition."

"That's nice," Will replied with a rather forced smile. He was anxious to start working before Laura showed up. Donning a pair of gloves, he walked over to the yard's edge, and knelt down beside a thick patch of weeds. He stabbed the ground with his weeder and penetrated down to the roots. Focusing on his task, Will quickly established a rhythm, digging under the offending growth with his tool, then pulling out the wild plant with his free hand. Before long, he had made his way to the front gate, but as luck would have it, he couldn't have reached that **juncture** at a more **inopportune** time.

With a screech of tires, a black BMW turned sharply into the driveway. Brady's BMW. Will broke out in a sweat. Out hopped Brady, waving toward the porch, where Laura was waiting. Will couldn't help but notice the jean miniskirt she was wearing, and how she eagerly greeted Brady. Her ponytail bobbed in sync with her easy **gait**. In barely a moment, the two had returned to the car and peeled out of the driveway—with barely a glance at Will.

Will watched in **disbelief** as the car disappeared. He knelt to resume his work, but wasn't finding the same groove as before. This time, when he jerked out the weeds, clumps of soil flew into his face.

Will forced himself to calm down. He blinked rapidly to **dislodge** a soil crumb and then began stripping the weeds. *She's just* *being friendly,* he assured himself hollowly. Perspiration was collecting on the back of his neck, and under the bright sun, he was feeling edgy, if not angry.

Just in time, Dr. Perez called out to him. "Want to take a break?"

A **hiatus** was just what Will needed. He joined Dr. Perez under an old gazebo on the side of the mansion. The octagonal frame, weathered by time, was supported by a **plethora** of vines that had become overgrown. The **panoply** provided much-needed shade.

"So how's the research going?" Will asked, sipping from the tall glass of iced tea Dr. Perez had poured.

"Interesting. Very interesting." Dr. Perez took a long swig from his own glass and smacked his **parched** lips. "Did you know there's no evidence that McAllister was even *on* the Titanic when it went down?"

"Really?" Will sat up, intrigued.

"There's a record of him purchasing a ticket, but no account of him actually boarding the ship. His name doesn't appear on the manifest." Perez hesitated. "Of course, that's not all that unusual. Some of the more wealthy people preferred **anonymity**—you know, a low profile. They might even have used an **alias**. But not McAllister. Everything he did, he did in a big way." Gesturing to the manor beside them as evidence, "Everything."

Will was troubled by what he heard. "I don't get it. McAllister had to have been on the Titanic. I mean, it's a known fact."

Dr. Perez raised his eyebrows. "Yes, it's an **enigma**. As with so many facets of his life, it's a **contradiction**." He cleared his throat. "Tell me, Will, why do you think McAllister left Red Fork to his servants?"

"Because he had so much and they had so little," Will replied, in almost a chant. It had been the first lesson he'd learned in civics class. Suspecting that Dr. Perez thought differently, he felt a bit uneasy. Was he suggesting that McAllister didn't have **altruistic** motives?

"Not the action of a robber-baron, is it?" Dr. Perez observed.

Will was puzzled. "What's a robber-baron?"

"Well, that's what a lot of people thought of them. **Affluent** men like Carnegie, Morgan, and McAllister. Some would say they were **entrepreneurs** who embodied the American dream—they rose from rags to riches. But the truth is, they did it at the expense of others." He paused to let Will digest his meaning. "At the end of the nineteenth century, they were the **titans** of business, but that's because they bribed government officials and were cruel to their workers. They were feared and **loathed** by those closest to them."

Clearly this was a personal subject for Dr. Perez. "Teddy Roosevelt called robber-barons the '**malefactors** of great wealth.' That means men like McAllister were rich criminals. They made their fortunes on the backs of their workers."

Will had never heard anyone **abase** Red Fork's guardian angel before, let alone question his moral character. "McAllister wasn't like that, though," he **beseeched**. "It makes no sense."

Dr. Perez knew full well that McAllister was **sacrosanct** here in Red Fork, but he reaffirmed his position. "It's a fact of the time, Will. It's because of these kinds of men that we have anti-trust laws now. To prevent the concentration of wealth and power in the hands of a few. And McAllister was definitely one of the few."

Will was not **assuaged**. "But those other men … I've heard their names attached to schools and—"

"Yes, you're right. They all donated vast amounts of money to set up universities, foundations, and concert halls. But they were actually paying to have their names attached to institutions that served a higher purpose. For them, all that **philanthropy** was great advertising. Really, none of them **evinced** the slightest concern for the common man." Will wanted to interrupt but Perez continued. "Yes, I know what you're thinking—none of them except for McAllister. You're wondering about Red Fork. So am I." He took another sip of his tea. "Truly, it is very odd. None of the other robber-barons made such a **munificent** gesture to their workers. And my research shows that McAllister was, for all intents and purposes, a sharp businessman who did well because he **exploited** his employees. But it's **paradoxical**, because he was also the generous **benefactor** of this town. And most significantly, he made that selfless gesture without knowing he was going to die." Perez **emphatically** thumped his palm on the arm of his chair. "Those other men donated their millions when they were on or near their deathbeds. McAllister, on the other hand, wrote his will while he was still a vibrant man. Unless he'd had some omen or **forethought** of his demise, he was still young enough to consider having children, in which case why not leave the estate to them?" Perez fell silent, clearly mystified by his own question. "These are the questions I've been grappling with. In his will, he showed genuine concern for his servants, but his prior actions paint a different picture altogether. No biographer has ever explored this **contradiction**. To me," Perez smiled, "That's what makes McAllister so interesting. After living the life of such an **egocentric**, he displayed uncommon compassion in what turned out to be one of his final acts."

Baffled, Will tried to reconcile what he knew about McAllister with this unsettling thesis. Could what he'd learned in school about McAllister be **fallacious**? He simply didn't know what to believe.

Dr. Perez realized that he'd upset Will, and his smile faded. His voice was apologetic as he tried to downplay his **speculation**, "I shouldn't have brought it up. I've got a lot more research to do. Maybe there's a good reason no other biographer has pursued this angle—maybe there's nothing to pursue." Rising from his seat, he topped off Will's glass. "I'll keep this pitcher full all day—make sure you take plenty of breaks. It's really hot today, and I don't want you getting dehydrated."

"Thanks," Will said gratefully, for both the iced tea and the change of subject. He gulped down his beverage and returned to his landscaping duties.

When Will reached the end of the lawn, he sighed. Now that he was done with the outer portion of the property, he'd have to **contend** with the weeds alongside the foundation of the house. That meant getting closer to Stone Manor. He looked up at the **imposing** hall and stared at the French doors through which he'd entered years ago. Apprehensively, he neared the mansion and started in on his chore, but when he neared the front door, shivers went down his spine. He was sure he could hear the wind whisper, "Lassiter."

The breeze **abated** before he could confirm what he'd heard, but the suspicion was enough to make him jump back. Whirling around, he spotted Dr. Perez **obliviously** applying lacquer to the armoire. Will exhaled slowly—everything was normal. The sun felt warm against his face as he quickly ripped out the remaining weeds.

At long last, Will had completed his work for the day. Stone Manor's yard was free of all **odious** growths and was ready for a landscaping makeover. He was gathering up his tools when the **staccato** honking of a car horn startled him.

He turned and recognized the BMW and its disagreeable owner. Pulling into the driveway, Brady got out, crossed over to the passenger door, and opened it for an appreciative Laura. She thanked him graciously as he kissed her on the cheek.

"I'll call you."

"Take care." She turned toward the front door, then noticed Will. "Hey," she said, waving.

A **tepid** nod was all Will could muster up. He shifted his attention back to Brady, who at this point had already gotten into his car. Worse, he had on a **smug** grin as he tore out of the driveway.

"This is fantastic!"

Will turned around to face a beaming Dr. Perez.

"You did an amazing job, Will! I didn't think it would be possible to accomplish all this in one day." He handed Will a check and patted him on the back. "Thank you. I see Laura was right as usual—you did a great job."

"You're welcome," Will murmured. He folded the check and tucked it away without even looking at the handsome sum Dr. Perez had awarded him—far more than what they'd originally negotiated. No, his mind was fixed elsewhere altogether. He was lost in the thought of Brady and Laura, together, laughing at him.

CHAPTER TEN

After dinner, Will retreated to his room. Locking the door, he gathered his drawing supplies and climbed onto his bed. He quickly sketched with his charcoal pencil, using short violent strokes, and before long, he had black smudges all over his arms. He was just starting to draw out the long shadows of the boathouse on the lake when he heard a knock.

"Will? Can I come in?" His closed door muffled Laura's voice. The **coquette** had returned to tease him again.

Will let a moment pass before answering. He wasn't eager to see her, but at the same time, he didn't want to be rude—he just wasn't of that **ilk**. Scanning the room for any dirty underwear, he shuffled over to unlock the door.

"Hi there." Laura was clad in the same tee she'd worn earlier in the day, though the miniskirt had been **supplanted** by green sweatpants. She pointed to some charcoal on his chin, "Nice goatee."

Silence. Finally, Laura cleared her throat. "So this is your room?" She crossed the threshold and walked right in.

Will allowed her to pass. "Yeah, it's where the magic happens." Given his current state of mind, it was his best stab at a joke. And judging from Laura's **subdued** reaction, it fell flat. He **reverted** to a more standard opener. "What's up?"

"Oh, my dad's doing research over at the historical society again, and … well, I didn't want to be in that house all by myself." Embarrassed, she added, "Wow, I sound like such a girl."

To this, Will could barely **elicit** a chuckle. He couldn't help but feel resentful about what went on today. Laura sensed the **acrimony**, too, and she had an **inkling** about what was causing it. "So, I hung out with Brady today." She wasn't one to beat around the bush. "He told me some pretty interesting things about you." She looked over to see his reaction.

"Oh yeah?" Outwardly, Will **exuded** indifference, but inside he cringed.

"He said you were a little off—kind of strange." Her steady **countenance** revealed no personal opinion. "That you're kind of a freak, the way you mow pictures into the grass and all that." Laura started to laugh.

Her reaction was all too familiar to Will. He'd heard the taunts, the chants, and the laughter before. Whenever his behavior

deviated from the norm—whether it was his unique lawn-cutting technique or his desire to leave Red Fork—he was called "weird," and his **peers** distanced themselves. Now it looked like Laura had joined them. Crushed and tired of this **ostracism**, Will tried to hide his **dejection**.

"Hey Will, what's wrong?"

The sudden concern in Laura's voice didn't fit with her cruel, **callous** laugh. Will was confused. Then he felt her hand on his shoulder.

"You feeling okay?"

Now he was just plain bewildered. Laura's concern seemed genuine, but at the same time, she was ridiculing him. Too tired to continue with this guessing game, he burst out, "Well, how do you expect me to feel after you insult me like that?"

"Insult you?" Now Laura was confused. "What are you talking ab—" Suddenly her eyes widened. "Oh no, Will, you've got it all wrong. I don't believe that stuff—I was only repeating Brady's words to show what a moron he is!" She struggled to find the right words.

Will looked at her blankly, in need of more convincing.

"Brady's the freak, Will." Laura let out a small laugh. "Like, what's up with that car?" She tilted her head in jest. "I mean, hello? Can you say *overcompensating*?" Encouraged by Will's breaking smile, she sassed on, "And you won't believe this—we stopped three times so he could clean the inside of the windshield. Three times!" Even Will couldn't keep from laughing at this tidbit.

Laura's shoulders slumped in relief, and she squeezed his shoulder again. "Listen," she spoke softly now, "You're the most normal guy I've met here. In fact, I think you're the only normal person in all of Red Fork." She winked, "It's everyone else who's a little strange!"

Will's **lugubrious** mood lifted. There was never any threat to their friendship; in fact, her **sojourn** with Brady had only solidified it. It looked like Laura even disliked Brady. The gleam came back in Will's eye. "You know, I always suspected I was a bit strange. But if you think I'm normal, then either you're right and I am," he pointed straight at Laura, "Or you're nuts."

The two doubled over in laughter. Laura liked Will's deadpan expression, and she was growing very comfortable with him. As their amusement **ebbed,** she began to survey his room, observing photographs and Matchbox cars, as well as an impressive collection of *National Geographic.* Her eyes landed on a pile of sketches.

She sifted through the drawings, examining each one closely. "Wow, did you do these? They're really good."

Will got to his feet and joined her.

"Did you ever think about applying to art school?"

As she rustled through the papers, a few drawings slid off the desk and onto the floor. As Laura leaned down to recover them,

Will got nervous. *Oh no, there's a sketch I just made of her standing in the window. I hope she doesn't see it.* The illustration would have been **innocuous**, were it not for the fact that the window resembled a mouth about to devour her.

Instead, Laura grabbed an old crayon drawing of Stone Manor and shuddered. Clearly the work of a child, the mansion was **circumscribed** with a moat of fire, and had red, eye-shaped windows along with sharpened fangs jutting out.

"I did that when I was 10," Will explained, silently recalling his trek into the manor. Drawing, he remembered, had been the only way to stop the trembling. "It's not very good."

"Oh yes it is!" Laura **averred**. "It totally captures Stone Manor." She set the drawing back on the desk and glanced guardedly out the window. "That place really creeps me out." She hesitated before going on. "There are some rooms I won't even go into. I know it sounds stupid, but I feel like I'm being watched. It just doesn't feel right there." She looked back up at Will, uncertain of his reaction.

"I can see how you'd feel that way." As usual, Will understated his views. The truth was, he was thrilled inside. *Hallelujah, it wasn't my imagination!* But still, not wanting to alarm her, he stayed quiet about his own childhood experience with Stone Manor.

Will couldn't help wonder just how similar their experiences were. "When you sleep now," he started **tentatively**, "Do you have—"

"Sleep?" Laura sneered. "I've barely slept a wink with all the weird creaks and noises at night. My dad says it's because the house is old and run down. He thinks he can renovate so it's not as rickety, but I'm not so sure. I mean, it's got landmark status and all, so I'm not sure how much he'd be allowed to do."

Caught off-guard by her **digression**, Will blinked to clear his head. "Um, that's not what I meant, but yeah, that's a bummer…." his voice trailed off as he wondered whether to finish his question. He had to know. "Do you have nightmares?"

Laura's voice was soft and **listless**, "I haven't dreamed at all since moving here."

Will was moved that she'd revealed such a **vulnerable** aspect of herself, and he wanted her to feel safe and comfortable with him now. They stood by the window together, their attention firmly fixed on Will's artwork.

*   *   *

The next couple of weeks passed without incident. The two friends met regularly and eagerly, whether at the Red Fork Café for lunch or at the lake for an afternoon dip. Laura enjoyed the rigorous **regimen** of doing laps, having been on the swim team in

Arizona. She wanted to regain her **endurance** and was determined to swim at least four times a week.

Their activities couldn't help but bring them closer, and Will couldn't have been happier. In fact, the way he saw it, there wasn't much missing from his life now. Except, of course, his friendship with Ty and Katie.

Will decided to try once more to pursue his friends. He'd known them too long to let them drop so quickly. He called Ty, thinking they could catch that upcoming double creature feature on TV. That offer was met with a **stilted** reply. He tried twice more and got a similar response. Ty was losing interest, in spite of how things had seemed that day they went sailing. *He probably just needs to spend time alone with Katie. It's always that way when you start dating someone.*

Will's own social calendar kept him very busy, for Laura had adopted the habit of dropping in whenever her father was out late. Since Dr. Perez was quite the dedicated researcher, that meant almost nightly. Usually, they watched TV or listened to music while drawing. Just as Laura was helping Will improve his swimming stroke, he was helping her develop her artistic ability. In only a few days, she'd graduated from **facile** stick figures to more complicated self-portraits. In fact, she was improving so quickly that Will joked about her "having a go with the lawn mower."

Occasionally, Laura would invite Will to hang out at the manor, but he'd always come up with an excuse not to go. One night, she called him on it. "Why don't you want to come over? Are you afraid of me?"

"Yeah, right!" Will laughed at the notion.

"So then are you scared of Stone Manor?" From the silence that followed, Laura knew she was right. "That's it, isn't it?" Laura suddenly realized what was going on. "You've never come inside. You always insist on waiting on the porch."

Will felt like a deer in headlights, and his throat went dry. *I've got to tackle this without giving everything away*, he thought, still sensitive to Laura's own fear of the manor. He pointed to his deflated football. "When I was in the manor years ago, looking for my football...." he turned his arm over, revealing the scar. "I got this."

"How?" She ran her fingers across the long blemish, remembering how touchy Will had been when she first asked about it.

"I don't know, actually. My arm got stuck somehow and as I was pulling it out, I got this. That's why I avoid the place. That would freak out any 10-year-old." He hoped Laura wouldn't press the issue further.

Laura frowned, knowing how much the wound must have hurt, and she rolled up her Capri pant leg. "See this? I stepped through a rotted floorboard and got this." She shook her head. "And that's not all. I'm not doing so well in that house," pointing to another nasty **contusion** above her right temple. "I fell down the stairs again the other day. The weirdest thing is, I wasn't even *going* down the stairs. I was just walking by the stairwell and the next thing I knew, I was falling. Almost like I was shoved or something."

"Shoved?" Will's body tensed up.

For a moment, Laura looked like she was about to **expound** on the incident, but then her focus shifted. "There was this other time, a *really* scary thing happened. My dad was outside, and I was in my room. And I swear, my door slammed shut by itself. It was probably the wind or something, but then the room started getting cold—I was literally shivering." Laura's eyes were wide now, and Will could tell she was reliving the whole experience. "I felt tight right here," putting her hand on her neck, "like someone was choking me. But only for a second. All of a sudden, the door flew back open from another gust of wind." She turned her troubled face to Will. "And if that's not strange enough, there was one more thing." She hesitated, now certain this all sounded **fabricated**. "I'm sure I heard a voice."

"A voice?" Will thought back to his own experience. *Was it a deep whisper? A woman's soothing voice? An ear-splitting cackle?* He wanted to ask, but he let Laura continue.

"Yeah," Laura's voice was soft, "For just a split second … I could've sworn it was my mother's voice," almost apologetic for the **implausible** story.

Of course, Will believed her every word. "What did she say?"

"I don't know. I think I was too shocked by the choking grip … I wasn't paying attention to the words. I just felt safe when I heard it."

Will touched her hand in **empathy**. *It's time—time to tell her about my ordeal in the manor.* At long last, he could share the one incident he'd been holding back, the milestone that shaped his life so dramatically. And for the first time, here was someone who would actually *believe* him. Will opened his mouth to speak, but a knock at the door cut him off.

"Laura? Honey, your dad's downstairs." Joanne's head peered inside the room. And with that, Laura hopped up from the desk chair and said her good-byes.

Left alone in his room, Will wanted to scream. His chance to **disclose** was gone. Depressed, he climbed into bed.

*   *   *

The wailing was more **audible** on this side of the door, but there was no sign of the crying baby. Before Will could go any farther, a dark, **formidable** figure reached out and grabbed him by the arm. Will's hand went numb.

The **incessant** crying grew louder as the two men struggled violently. At one point, Will caught a glimpse of his face: long brown hair, **angular** face, and square jaw. And piercing black eyes.

Sharp waves of pain came on. A **serrated** blade had sunk deep into Will's forearm. With all his strength, Will yanked it away, and rammed the man into a dark corner. Struggling to wrap his T-shirt around his wounded arm, he ran out the door, barely stopping to catch his breath. When he finally reached safe ground, he saw a familiar sight: the same jagged cut that had disfigured him years ago. Warm blood oozed out.

CHAPTER ELEVEN

The throbbing jolted Will awake. It was the first time in years that his arm had ached, and, given this latest nightmare, it seemed a **foreboding** sign. Sitting up, he replayed the **surreal** events of his dream, trying to **ascribe** them possible meanings. He was abruptly interrupted.

A series of rapid explosions boomed outside. This startled Will, and he nervously craned his neck out the window to investigate. To his relief, the real **culprits** were his 12-year-old neighbor Josh Anderson and Josh's friend Zach, who were lighting firecrackers in the street. *Of course*, Will thought: *This is the Fourth of July.*

He showered and dressed quickly, moving on to the **requisite** All-American breakfast. Today's scrambled eggs and sausage were prepared by his mother, and Will was grateful for it. Still chewing the last morsel, he flew out the door over to the mansion.

"Hey Laura, do you want to go to the parade togeth—?" Will stopped short when he saw Dr. Perez at the door. "Oh, hi, Dr. Perez."

Dr. Perez called up to Laura, then faced Will again, leaning casually against the doorframe. "Going to the parade today?"

"Yup. There's also a huge carnival. This year, the whole thing will be even bigger, since it's the town's hundredth anniversary." He was referring to the centennial celebration of the establishment of Red Fork. Coincidentally, July Fourth marked not only the anniversary of American independence but also the date—exactly 100 years ago today—on which McAllister began building his estate. The occasion called for a special **jubilee**. "You should check it out."

"Maybe I will," Dr. Perez grinned at Will's excitement. "You and Laura have fun." As he spoke, his daughter slid past him and joined Will on the porch.

The two soon made their way over to McAllister Boulevard and navigated the parade's staging area. Once at the park, they staked out a spot with a clear view of the parade, and within minutes, Ty and Katie arrived. It had been some time since they had last seen each other.

"Will, have you grown?" Katie offered, trying to make light of their recent **estrangement**. Will appreciated her lighthearted attempt to **alleviate** the awkwardness. "No, but I'm married now with four kids."

Will's wisecrack drew grins all around and dissolved any lingering tension. As Katie brought Laura up to speed on the town gossip, Ty took Will aside. They stepped over to the statue of McAllister.

"I guess you figured out that Katie and I are, well, you know...." Ty looked to Will to complete his thought.

"Going out?"

"Yeah." Ty fidgeted, twirling a small branch in his hands. "It just sort of happened, and we wanted to see if it was going anywhere before we told anyone." Ty looked for any hint of disappointment. "That's why we've both been busy."

"I figured as much. And am happy for you guys."

This wasn't entirely true, Will thought. After all, Ty and Katie's getting together had only made Will feel **alienated** from his friends. But Will wanted no more **antipathy** among them, so he put on his best face. "And I'm happy that's why I haven't seen you two around. I was starting to think I smelled or something."

"Well, to be honest," Ty said with a straight expression, "you do give off a rather strange odor. I didn't want to say anything, but...." Will began to turn red. "Gotcha! Boy, you're **gullible**." Ty howled with laughter.

The parade had just started. A fife player, a revolutionary soldier, and a snare drummer were the first to arrive, followed by George Washington, Ben Franklin, and other founding fathers, in the form of a local acting **troupe**.

Among these patriots was a **gaunt**-faced Algernon McAllister. His Victorian-era clothing an **anachronism** alongside Thomas Jefferson's eighteenth-century garb, he towered over the other actors. The real McAllister had been a lofty six feet tall, and his success had come in no small part from his commanding presence.

Watching from the park, Will felt a flash of **déjà vu**. The tall figure with the flowing brown hair looked familiar, but a *Happy 100th Birthday, Red Fork!* banner interrupted his thoughts. The background strains of "You're a Grand Old Flag" was **lamentably** out of tune, and Will's ears were ringing at the **discordant** racket.

An armada of floats rolled by. The first, sponsored by the local Boy Scouts troop, represented the signing of the Declaration of Independence. **Subsequent** ones re-enacted the flag-raising on Iwo Jima and Neil Armstrong's walk on the moon. For full effect, this last one was decorated with gray spray-painted tissue paper as the **lunar** surface.

Sportive performers followed, performing **impromptu** pranks and skits—Ray among them, on stilts. Juggling two balls and a bowling pin, his arms and legs were synchronized perfectly in an impressive display of **eurythmics**. Closing the procession were a fire engine and an old steam-engine locomotive, fashioned with another McAllister look-alike and several small children.

Soon, the **revelry** shifted toward the park, where parade organizers had set up a **pavilion** for food. The vast array of food was attacked within minutes: hamburgers, hot dogs, chicken and baby back ribs; buttery corn and fresh-baked rolls; chocolate **confections; savory** fixings and fries; manicotti, courtesy of Sal and Marie; and sparkling sodas for all. A **bustle** of activity filled the area.

No sooner had the four friends started eating, than Brady **sauntered** over, hidden behind stylish sunglasses. He went straight for Laura.

"I've got my jet-ski with me," his voice was smooth and **haughty**. "I was thinking we could go for a spin." He glanced in Will's direction, looking for a reaction.

Laura bit into her cheeseburger. "That sounds like fun, but I don't think so." Bits of beef **inadvertently** spewed onto Brady's name-brand sandals. No doubt, her rejection wasn't taken well. Brady took off his sunglasses and stared directly at Laura. "Oh, I meant after you're finished eating."

With a quick flick of her head, Laura **rebuffed** his advance. "Listen, Brady, I'm not interested. Not in your jet-ski, not in your BMW, and not in you. Please leave." She was **vociferous** in her request.

Four pairs of eyes zeroed in as Brady turned flush red. He backed off, trying to **exude** indifference. "Your loss. But I can't imagine why you'd rather hang out with these losers. Unless," raising an eyebrow, "you've got more in common with them than I thought."

Laura waited until Brady was out of earshot before responding to his **callow** remark. "What a little weasel!" Will was elated, thrilled by her **sagacious** ability to see through to the real person.

Feeling ten-feet tall, Will walked the rest of the carnival hand-in-hand with Laura. The sense of **assimilation** that always **eluded** him now seemed within reach. Watching Ty and Katie together, Will could for the first time relate to their happiness.

Making their way through the entire party, Will and Laura sampled apple pie and homemade preserves, and tried their luck at the ring toss. They even stopped at the Historical Society booth, where Daniel Bell stood ready to answer questions and show off relics he'd encased in glass. Will **perused** the items and discovered McAllister's birth certificate, along with the famous last will and **testament** in which he gave his estate to his servants.

"Here's the original deed to your house," Bell said to Laura, pointing to a yellowed piece of paper. "If your father would like, I can make a copy of it."

"Thanks, I'll let him know." She pulled Will away from the booth. "That guy is really odd."

"The Society is his life," Will nodded, his tone sympathetic. "He's not married or anything, so it's all he's got. I guess he gets a little carried away."

"A little?" Laura blurted out. "That guy needs to find a hobby. Or get a pet."

As they snickered, Ty approached them. "Hey guys, I'm entering the pie-eating contest. Come over and cheer me on!" He rubbed his stomach. "I'm thinking this is my event—I've always been good at eating!"

Will and Laura followed him to a large airy tent and joined Katie in the audience. When Ty's name was called, they cheered loudly as he stood up and joined the other contestants. *What a surprise that Ray's up there,* thought Will.

Judging from the **corpulence** of their opponents, neither of the Martin brothers seemed to stand much of a chance. They'd have to eat as many cherry pies as possible in five minutes. Ty was flanked by Harold Dittlemeyer, the 400-pound town **bursar**, and Stacy Oglethorpe, from the McAllister College women's basketball team. Ty **suppressed** a smile, remembering that Stacy had been his brother's prom date. Three seats away, Ray was sandwiched between the only twins in town, Richard and Roger Goodwin, who, at age 11, were already twice the size of other kids their age.

After thanking a local bakery for donating the pies, the mayor launched the timer with a ceremonial flourish. Immediately, Ty grabbed a fistful of pie and stuffed it in his mouth, followed by another, and then another. His mouth and chin stained with the bright red filling, he pushed on. Next to him, Harold Dittlemeyer adopted a different strategy, burying his face into the crust and inhaling the pie's innards without even bothering to chew.

When the buzzer sounded the end of the contest, Ty slumped back in his chair and triumphantly eyed the five empty pie tins before him. Impressive as his feat was, it paled in comparison to the performances of his fellow **contenders**. Stacy had eaten seven pies, and the Goodwin twins had each polished off eight. But even their extraordinary intake was only sufficient for third place. Harold Dittlemeyer had wolfed down 10 pies, an accomplishment made all the more remarkable by the fact that he didn't spill anything on his white dress shirt. Still, even he finished second to Ray, who disposed of a whopping eleven pies. The onlookers cheered for all six contestants and their awe-inspiring show of **gluttony**.

The **culmination** of the day was a huge fireworks celebration. As the night sky filled with color, "oohs" and "ahhs" could be heard all around. This was the perfect time for Will and Laura to **surreptitiously** steal away.

Finding a **remote** area of the beach, Will gazed at Laura. She trusted him **implicitly**. At last, his dream had become a reality. Their **amorous** connection was real. Without saying a word, their lips met. It was the warm, tingly sensation only a first kiss could produce. The moment might have gone on forever, Will later thought, were it not for the blast that forced them apart. They watched in horror as the boathouse exploded in a bright orange fireball.

CHAPTER TWELVE

The fireworks display came to an immediate halt, but despite its **cessation**, the night sky still glowed. The flames' **monochromatic** hue reflected off the lake and into the burning eyes of frightened spectators. The townspeople rushed to cover their heads with beach towels to shield themselves from the falling embers. Hysterical parents struggled to break through the frenzied surge, coughing as they screamed out to children lost in the dark smoke. The billowing cloud of soot **diffused** the flashing glow of a fire truck as it sped toward the chaotic scene.

The fire was quickly engulfing the building, intensifying in force and **magnitude**. By the time the firefighters arrived, it had grown steadily. To make matters worse, a water line to the fire truck broke, and their initial attempt to douse the flames proved **abortive**. The **beleaguered** firefighters began the **antiquated** system of passing buckets of lake water, which proved temporarily successful until the bad connection could be fixed.

Will and Laura remained on the beach, a safe distance from the fire. They could only watch in shock as the **conflagration** was battled. Their romantic **tryst**, which just minutes ago had **culminated** in that magnificent kiss, was now a distant memory.

At long last, the fire was contained and extinguished. Creases of worry etched onto their faces, concerned residents waited for some official news. Finally, the sheriff emerged from his hastily constructed command post under the same tent that only hours ago had housed the pie-eating contest. With the fire chief at his side, he addressed the crowd in a slow drawl.

"Well, I'm happy to report that there were no casualties, except for the boats inside. At first we thought some **errant** fireworks had landed on the structure, but it doesn't look like that's the case." The sheriff fell silent.

"Then what was it, Fred?" Dolores's irritated voice rang out.

"I don't want to say anything now that I might have to **repudiate** later on," the sheriff replied stiffly. His careful choice of words signified a shift from his normally **amicable** tone to the more authoritative and **aloof** voice of a government official. "Mr. Mayor?"

The mayor joined the sheriff in front of the **garrulous** citizens. "Now I'm sure you all have a lot of questions. I know I do. But we need some time to come up with answers. After all, it's only been a few minutes since it happened. I've **convened** an emergency meeting of the town council and hope to have some answers within the next couple of hours. You're welcome to come, but for now, please return to your homes."

People were apprehensive. They dawdled nervously for a short time and then began to scatter, fanning out across McAllister Boulevard and heading for the **byways** where they lived. The **acrid**, smoky odor of the blaze still hung in the air. Will and Laura made their way toward Stone Manor. When they arrived, they hugged.

Laura buried her face in Will's neck. After a long silence, she leaned up. "I was having a great time, you know."

Will cupped her cheek in his hand. "I'm gonna go change, and then I'll come back over and we'll go to the meeting together. Okay?"

In **tacit** approval, she smiled and slipped into the mansion, and Will jogged over to his house. No sooner had he stepped in the door than his parents **accosted** him.

"Where were you?" Joanne asked in a **shrill** tone.

Will immediately sought to **appease** their worry. "I was on the beach with Laura. It was such a madhouse that we decided to stay put until it was all over. At that point, I couldn't find you guys, so we just came back here."

Visibly relieved, Ken squeezed his son's shoulder and asked if he had seen what happened.

Will shook his head. He remembered what had preoccupied him at the moment of the blast, and had to **suppress** a smile.

"We looked all over for you. When we heard that no one was hurt, we came back here figuring you'd already be back. Then, when you weren't, we started to worry."

Joanne collapsed on the sofa. "But here you are now. Thank goodness!" She wrapped an afghan around her shoulders. "Now do you see why we worry about you traveling far from home?"

Will wasn't in the mood to start in on college again. *Just let her **reactionary** comment pass. Don't get started with her.* "I'm going to wash up before we head to the meeting." He ran upstairs and took a quick shower. The hot water was a welcome **anodyne**, soothing away the tension from his body.

The Lassiters and Perezes all went together to Town Hall. By the time they arrived, most seats had been filled, so they stood at the back, waiting for word of the latest **tidings**. After a few minutes, the mayor ambled to the **rostrum**, his considerable **girth** causing the old floorboards to creak. **Gavel** to the **podium**, he leaned in to the microphone.

"If it's all right with the council, we'll **dispense with** the usual formalities. I'll get straight to the point. The cause of the boathouse fire has been determined: A gas line under the structure ruptured, and the **flammable** substance blew up when it came in contact with the fireworks. Any questions?"

At least 20 hands shot up, accompanied by a gush of **dissonant** voices. The **queries** themselves were virtually incomprehensible. The mayor raised his arms for quiet but was ignored, and had no choice but to holler for quiet. His voice had the tone of an irritated parent to **impudent** children: "I will address your concerns, one at a time!"

He first pointed to Wendy Oliver, who ran the rec center at the boathouse. She asked him to clarify which gas line he was talking about. With assistance from the sheriff and fire chief, they explained that a line had been found under the boathouse—a line that must have been there for at least 90 years. Somehow, it was turned on. And oddly, they never knew this line existed.

This is beginning to sound a lot like what happened at Sal's, thought Will. *Could there be a **correlation**?*

Others in the audience had been thinking the same thing. "It's possible," the fire chief noted **dubiously**, "but we're still operating under the **hypothesis** that that accident was caused by a defective oven."

Sal instantly bolted up from his chair. "That's not true!" he exclaimed, **adamant**. "There's nothing wrong with my ovens. I think the mayor is right—it must be another gas line." He started to sit, then stopped in mid-air, addressing the **rapt** crowd, "By the way, Sal's grand re-opening is tomorrow, and it's even better than before!"

Leave it to Sal to plug his restaurant at a time like this. Still, it provided some **levity** to the proceedings, and people chuckled at the **opportunist's** nerve. After the laughter died down, Daniel Bell stood up. "I want to point out that Sal's Pizzeria and the boathouse are both parts of the original estate. They are historical landmarks, and I'm *very* distressed by the destruction that's taking place."

"Hey, maybe we've got an arsonist on our hands," came a voice from the back. This suggestion **engendered** further **speculation**.

Others, Dolores among them, took a more **parochial** approach. Standing up from her chair, she cut off another resident midsentence and, in her usual **brusque** manner, **interjected**, "I think we're all skirting the real issue. This town has been peaceful for as long as I can remember. But now with these accidents, you have to ask what's different? What's new here?"

Without even looking in their direction, Will knew that Dolores was referring to Dr. Perez and Laura. So did the rest of the room, which erupted in another spate of arguments. Many people demanded she **recant** her suggestion, though a few agreed with her **censorious** remark. Exhibiting the same type of **xenophobia**, one old man went so far as to proclaim, "These things only started happening after *they* showed up and moved into Stone Manor."

His **blatant** accusation **fomented** a full-scale shouting match among audience members, and as the town council meeting degraded into a **fracas**, the mayor surrendered to the uproar and left the stage. Taking their cue from the mayor's hastened exit, Ken, Joanne, and Dr. Perez tugged their kids out the back door.

CHAPTER THIRTEEN

Will spent the night tossing restlessly in bed. He couldn't shake the events from the meeting and the ensuing trip home. After the gathering had broken down to a **raucous** debate, he had walked with Laura while his parents followed with Dr. Perez. Numbed by the accusations and **innuendo** that had surfaced in the hall, nobody said a word.

It was almost eleven in the morning when he emerged groggy and bleary-eyed. Off-balance from his **fitful** sleep, Will couldn't concentrate on breakfast: not on the newspaper, not on pouring the maple syrup, not on drinking his juice. A knock on the door jolted him out of his stupor, and when he looked up, Laura was waving from the other side of the screen.

"Good morning, dear," Joanne said, letting Laura in. "Can I fix you some waffles?"

From her **ambivalence**, Will knew something was wrong. They waited until Joanne left the room to talk.

Apparently, Dr. Perez had said something strange that morning—something about Laura staying out of the house until he got back.

"He said he wanted to check on the 'structural **integrity**' of the place. But I could tell he was lying. He always stutters when he lies. Today, he was stuttering like crazy." Her lower lip trembled. "Why would he lie to me?"

Will tried to soothe her. It didn't sound like a totally unreasonable request to him. Both explosions had taken place in really old buildings, and maybe Dr. Perez just wanted to make sure those same gas lines weren't running under Stone Manor. "Actually, I think all the original houses from the estate should be checked, including mine."

Laura sighed. "Maybe you're right. I guess with everything that's been going on, I'm feeling a little sensitive."

Although he'd calmed her down, Will still had his own reservations about Dr. Perez's strange behavior. *Given all of Laura's* **mishaps***, maybe it's not the physical structure he's worried about; maybe he's really worried about something less* **tangible***.* Will's mind didn't wander too long, though, as a car horn summoned them outside.

An old Volkswagen Rabbit was parked in the driveway, Ty sitting proudly behind the wheel next to Katie. "I passed!" he shouted, holding up his temporary driver's license. "And on my first try, too!"

"That's great." Will offered, shaking his friend's hand through the open window. "So this is your car now?"

"Yeah. Since Ray just bought the truck, I got this." He revved the four-cylinder engine, producing a high-pitched whine that sounded eerily similar to Will's lawn mower. "Hop in."

As Will and Laura squeezed into the back, the small vehicle groaned under the extra weight. Ty shifted the gear into reverse and slowly backed down the driveway. It was the first time he was driving his compact at full capacity, and the extra passengers made him cautious.

The four friends drove around Red Fork for an hour or so, and Ty grew more comfortable zipping around at the wheel. His turns became so fast and sharp that Will kept slamming into Laura in the back seat.

Remembering Sal's **blatant** promotion of the grand re-opening, they decided to go for pizza. Balloons adorned the **façade** of the restaurant as Frank Sinatra blared from speakers. The red and white-checkered tablecloths were unchanged, and most important, Sal was still enthusiastically flinging dough in the air. Repainted and refurnished, the only evidence of damage in the place was the tarp that covered a hole in kitchen wall.

Soon, however, Laura became uncomfortable. "I feel like everyone's staring at me," she whispered to her friends. "After last night, I feel funny being here." She glumly picked a piece of pepperoni off her slice.

"You mean Dolores? Don't pay attention to her. She's in her own world—she actually believes that the president is a Martian who wants to take over the earth. She's **leery** of NASA." Ty laughed, shaking his head at the notion.

"And she's the target of a lot of jokes," Katie added. "Behind her back, people call her 'Da Lunatic' instead of 'Dolores.' There are a couple of other **buffoons** like her around, and they're always **outspoken** at those meetings." Seeing that Laura was beginning to relax, Katie went on. "One time, she went on this **tirade** about squirrels. She said they were eating the molding off her house so she called for an **edict** condemning them to extinction."

The **anecdote** made Laura smile, and the tension lifted. As the friends toasted their driving **tyro**, Sal came over and, in a **jocular** tone, welcomed them back. Laura grinned, grateful that his warmth expressed no **enmity**.

"We're glad you and Marie are okay and the restaurant is open again," said Katie. "How are the renovations going?"

"Very well!" He gestured toward the canvas separating them from the carpenters. "As you can see, we've still got more to do, but in the end we'll be better off. I'm getting a jukebox so you kids can hear what *real* music sounds like. Any of you ever hear of Frank Sinatra? Tony Bennett? Dean Martin?" Surprised at their nods, he **bellowed** to the kitchen, "Hey, another pie over here!"

"See, Laura? You've got nothing to worry about," Will **reiterated**. "If Sal really thought you had something to do with the fire, he wouldn't have been so nice."

Laura smiled easily now. "You're right. I'm just being paranoid." She took another bite of her slice. "This really *is* the best pizza I've ever had."

A few minutes later, their second pizza arrived and was quickly devoured. The friends had **voracious** appetites, and they ate until their bellies were **distended**. Laura licked marinara sauce off her fingers as she turned to Ty and Katie. "So what are you guys going to do after you graduate?"

"McAllister College." They replied in unison.

Ty was the first to explain. "I'm going to take business and computer science. I want to start my own software company." Known as the computer geek in school, Ty had already built his own PC from scratch and was in charge of maintaining the official Red Fork website.

Katie was going for prelaw. "Maybe I'll be the town's first female mayor." And with the **artfulness** of a politician, she stuck out her arm to shake Laura's hand. "And I assume I can count on your support?"

Laura was impressed. "Wow, you guys know exactly what you want. I've been traveling so much over the past few years, I'm really not sure anymore."

Katie seemed genuinely surprised that Laura was so undecided. She glanced at Will and noted, "Well, you're not the only one."

"Yeah, there must be something in the water on your block," Ty grinned. "But hey, the world needs dreamers."

"And registered voters," Katie quipped.

After lunch, the drive around town was short. Red Fork was hardly a metropolis, and the friends grew bored cruising down the same streets. Less than 30 minutes later, they'd all had enough.

Not much at home interested Will either. In front of the television, he flipped mindlessly between channels. An hour or so later, he looked over his mowing schedule. Then, trying to sketch, he wasn't inspired.

Fortunately, Will spotted Laura out the window. She was standing on her front porch. *Dr. Perez still isn't home?* he thought. He ran down the stairs and, as he approached her, felt **sheepish** for not realizing she was outside all the while. Laura looked **forlorn**, though her face lit up quickly on seeing him.

Back at Will's house, they plopped onto the living room sofa. They talked first of driving, with Will cataloging his numerous failed attempts to get his license, then moved on to their friends. **Perplexed**, Laura sat up. "It's so weird to me that Ty and Katie are going to McAllister College. They're both smart—they could do so much better." She turned to Will, blushing. "I'm sorry. I don't mean to sound critical. I know they're your friends and all, and I really do like them a lot."

In fact, Will welcomed her **frankness.** "Don't worry about it. I feel the same way. It *is* weird. It's like no one ever wants to leave Red Fork, like it's some kind of **utopia.**" Will looked down at his hands. "I'm the only exception: I can't wait to get out of here."

He felt calmer as soon as he'd uttered these last words. He'd just revealed one of his most guarded secrets—a confession that until now had isolated him from his parents and his peers. But Laura, of all people, must recognize how **insular** the residents here were.

Before she had a chance to reply, Will's mother stepped into the room, with an offer of fresh vegetable fajitas. In between bites at the dinner table, Will's father asked Laura what she thought of the town.

"It's your typical tight-knit community," Laura replied easily. "Everyone knows each other, so it's like it's one big family. Of course, some of them are the cousins you can't stand," **alluding** to the feisty Dolores. "But for the most part, I really like the closeness."

Joanne agreed with her **assessment.** "You're absolutely right. But some people," fixing her eyes on Will, "are never satisfied with what they have."

Will shot a glance at Laura. *See, even in my own house, I'm alone in my view.*

Hours passed, and Dr. Perez had still not returned. Laura dozed off, her head nestled in Will's shoulder. Not wanting to awaken her with any sudden movements, Will **eschewed** the idea of retiring to his room and opted to stay put, resting his head against the plush cushions and snuggling closer to Laura's warm body.

CHAPTER FOURTEEN

Sunlight streamed into the living room and onto the couch where Will and Laura were sleeping. The **effulgent** light gradually stirred them, their first moments a bit awkward.

In her semiconscious state, Laura smiled radiantly, then rubbed her eyes to wipe away the residues of sleep. Feeling uncharacteristically shy about their **propinquity**, she sprang to the opposite side of the sofa.

Will, on the other hand, was **emboldened** by their night together. He stretched his arms into the air, yawned, and stood up. "Can I make you some breakfast?" he offered, with an **urbane** manner not typical of him. Laura **tottered** a bit before rushing off to the bathroom, and within minutes, she emerged more alert. Straight away, she excused herself to run home.

Will watched through a window as Laura ran next door. Calling out for her father, she circled the house. At one point she disappeared around the back, only to emerge a minute later. **Lachrymose**, she headed back to Will's house.

"I don't know where he is," she said, pulling open the screen door and stepping into the foyer. She fought back tears. "His car is there, but that doesn't mean much since he walks everywhere."

Will tried to think of something comforting, offering that maybe he was just fast asleep.

"You think?" Laura tried to look hopeful. "Well," she hesitated, "then, will you do me a favor?"

She looked down awkwardly. She knew it was asking a lot of Will, and the **ramifications** of her request were **palpable**. "If he's just sleeping, or if he fell down somewhere—then I need to go look for him and find out for sure. Some of the wood in that house *is* pretty rotted." Laura bit her lip, "But, I can't go alone. The last thing he said to me was to stay out of the house. If I'm going to break my word, at least I'd feel less **culpable** if you were with me."

Dread came over Will. Laura was asking for the impossible. *How can I go back there?* Shifting uncomfortably, he **ruminated** the point and nearly refused her. But knowing how badly she needed his support—and how badly he wanted to give it to her— he made up his mind to **quash** his obsessive fear. He agreed to go with her before his **phobia** got the better of him.

As they passed across the threshold of Stone Manor, Will felt almost nauseous, but he continued on in. From the vestibule, they entered a **commodious** room with doors to the left and right. An elegant staircase curved up to the second floor and around a delicate glass chandelier. Laura called for her father, her voice echoing in the large chamber.

Searching the first floor, they passed from the dining room to the **voluminous** kitchen, and back to the parlor. Will studied the animal heads mounted on the wall, surprised by how homey the room felt. *If we replace the stuffed moose head with a large screen TV, this could well be a **precursor** to the modern den.* Stopping in front of an armchair in faded velvet, he could picture McAllister as a young man: cigar in one hand, literary volume in the other.

Dr. Perez's bedroom was next. This room, too, couldn't have changed much from when it was first built. Though the walls looked like tin, they were actually imprinted mauve squares on sage green circles. The undisturbed bed was enough for Laura to know that her father hadn't slept there overnight. Before leaving, she snatched his journal off the nightstand.

There was one last room they needed to search. It was **remote**, at the top of a wobbly flight of stairs. With low, slanted ceilings, it had accumulated years' worth of cobwebs and dust. An old wooden wheelchair stood in the corner, and Will knew that this must have belonged to Helena Ross when she lived at the manor.

Its **meticulous** details were **indicative** of the fact that the room must have once served an important purpose: an oak cutout of nuts and berries adorned the top of the walls, and satin drape remnants filled the windows. As for the view, one could see all of

Red Fork—polo fields and stables to the north, and McAllister Boulevard and the lake to the south. *What a great room to draw in,* thought Will. *It has such creative **fodder**.*

Yet the room was eerie and the two friends felt uncomfortable being there. Even the air was abnormally heavy. They stood admiring the **panorama**, desperate for a **novel** idea on where to search next. And that's when things started to get downright alarming. First, they felt a distinct chill. And then, **preceded** by a creaking noise, the wheelchair rolled slowly across the room. It dug a straight tract for several feet and came to a leisurely halt. Not waiting to see what might happen next, Will and Laura bolted, terrified, down three flights of stairs and out of the house.

Will panted, trying to sound convincing. "Your father is definitely not in there." He wanted to **dissuade** Laura in case she had lingering doubts. Laura nodded **vehemently**, speechless. At a loss for what to do next, the logical thing seemed to be to ask Will's dad for advice.

Ken and Joanne were gardening in the backyard. When Will explained Laura's situation—that Dr. Perez had been missing for over 24 hours—Ken became **resolute**. "We should tell the sheriff." In seconds, they were off to the police station.

They found Fred Tompkins behind his desk gnawing on a stick of cherry licorice. Ken started to speak but was distracted by the rod of candy dangling from the sheriff's mouth.

"Oh, sorry." The **portly** Tompkins stuffed the last of the sweet into his mouth. "I'm trying to quit smoking. Heard licorice was a good substitute."

Three of his visitors **inadvertently** dropped their eyes to the sheriff's pronounced gut, wondering whether candy was indeed a wise replacement. Only Laura still gazed levelly into his face. He listened attentively as she described her father's disappearance.

"How long has he been gone?" Tompkins asked, reaching for another licorice stick.

From the **innumerable** police dramas he watched on TV, Will gathered that the sheriff wouldn't file a missing persons report until 48 hours had elapsed, so he **embellished** their story: "Day before yesterday." He wanted the police to start searching immediately.

"Two days, eh?" The sheriff glanced at his calendar and chuckled, knowing exactly where Will was going. "Too bad. We could have started looking yesterday."

Laura moved quickly to **amend** Will's **fabricated** timeline. "Actually, the last time I saw my dad was yesterday morning."

"Okay, now we're getting somewhere. You play fair with me, and I'll play fair with you." Tompkins reached into a drawer, pulled out a form, and inserted it into an old Smith-Corona typewriter. The computer next to it looked seldom-used.

"Name?"

"Dr. Octavio Perez."

"Age?"

"47."

Laura proceeded to answer all the **pertinent** questions about her father—his height, weight, and general description.

"You're new to Red Fork, right? Where were you living before?" When Laura told him they'd moved from Chicago, he **recoiled** in distaste. "Chicago? There's a crime-ridden city," he miffed. "How long did you live there?"

"Not very long." Laura **recounted** the numerous places they had resided since her mother passed away and the reasons for each move.

"My, you've led an interesting life, haven't you?" he leaned back. "What made your father decide to move here of all places?"

This was starting to sound like an interrogation. Both Will and his parents said nothing, though it was obvious Laura was getting frustrated. Her reply had an edge to it. "He's writing a book about Algernon McAllister." She drew out McAllister's name, hoping her mention of Red Fork's **apotheosis** might soften the sheriff.

No such luck; his **patronizing** tone continued. "A book? But there are already a ton of books about him." At Laura's silence, he swiveled idly in his chair. "Did the **eminent** doctor have any enemies?"

"Look, are you going to help us or not?" Will **interjected** impatiently. He started to rise, but his parents restrained him.

"Son, I advise you to sit down and keep quiet." Tompkins turned back to Laura.

So angered by the **inference**, Laura could barely contain herself. "No enemies!" She **adamantly refuted** the sheriff. The **astringent** questioning was beginning to erode her **composure**, and she had to work hard to maintain her **equanimity**. Calming herself, she **qualified** her remark: "Sir, my father is the most harmless guy in the world. He's an academic—a bookworm. He has no enemies whatsoever." She glared back at the sheriff, waiting to see how he would twist that statement.

"I find it highly **suspect** that your father would disappear in the middle of our investigation." Laura, he felt, was **rationalizing** her father's behavior, and he seemed intent on **upbraiding** her.

"Just what are you **insinuating**?" Laura replied.

"The boathouse explosion and the fire at Sal's. Contrary to our public announcements, we have very good reason to believe these incidents were started deliberately." He watched as the **tacit** meaning behind his words dawned on Laura's face. "Can you tell me where your father was at the time of each incident?"

Incensed by the implied accusation, Laura sputtered incoherently several times before managing to compose a complete sentence. "My father would never do any of those things!" She was stunned the sheriff would even dare *suggest* that her father had committed the crimes and **absconded** from town. "All I know is that my father is missing," Laura's voice grew

belligerent, turning the heads of deputies around the office, "And all you seem to care about is finding an easy scapegoat so you can sit back here and pig out on your stupid licorice." She angrily bolted out of her chair, knocked the candy jar over with a sweeping stroke of her arm and jeered, "Why don't you do your job, Slim?"

Laura turned on her heels to stalk away, but the sheriff, showing unusual **dexterity**, jumped up and blocked her path. **Defiant** at first, Laura reluctantly slumped back down into her seat.

Tompkins attempted a **conciliatory** tone: "Since Laura is considered a minor, she can't stay in that big house all alone. Now, the missus and I can put her up—"

"That's okay!" Ken piped in, saving the day. "She's more than welcome to stay with us."

Tompkins's shoulders sagged in relief. "Thank you. I think that would be the most comfortable arrangement."

Yeah, for you, Will seethed as they rose to take their leave.

Laura wasn't feeling terribly hopeful. For the rest of the afternoon, they stayed close to the phone, but by nightfall, there was still no news. Ken's triumphant spaghetti with basil marinara sauce even went unapplauded. Worn from the strain of the day, Laura went to bed on a cot in the den, and within seconds, was asleep.

The ordeal had the opposite effect on Will. His mind was **inundated** with **conjecture**. There were so many things going on in Red Fork—accidents, disappearances. *What is happening?* He turned on his side to face Stone Manor. The house appeared to glow; it looked deceptively innocent.

The low murmurs from his parents' bedroom didn't help. Doing what the typical curious teenager would do, Will leaned in to eavesdrop. He could hear only snippets of their conversation.

"Do you think Laura's father had anything to do with the explosions? It hadn't occurred to me, but it's awfully coincidental that he's disappeared." Joanne paused. "He just doesn't seem the type, though. He's so mild-mannered."

The voices started fading, and Will pressed his ear closer.

"I don't know. I'm starting to think maybe it was McAllister's ghost. Laura said the last place she saw him was in the house…."

"That house does have a history," Joanne agreed. "Johnny Gunn, Helena Ross…"

"We may be adding 'Perez' to that list soon." Ken's voice was gloomy.

Will was stunned by his parents' suspicions. For years they had **derided** the superstitions about Stone Manor as silly. It was what they'd told him after he'd cut his arm all those years ago. Of all people, Will least expected them to take the legend of Stone Manor seriously. *But if they believed in it all along, why weren't they more supportive when I came home with the bloody arm?*

CHAPTER FIFTEEN

The Lassiter household was quiet late into the morning, until the clatter of pots roused the two teenagers. Will padded into the room, **debilitated** by his restless sleep. Yesterday's events all seemed **surreal**.

Will scowled at his cheery mother as he entered the kitchen. If nothing else, he was **lucid** about what he'd overheard his parents say. Laura entered a short time later, a **vexed** expression on her face. The **grievous** situation with her father was taking its toll.

Fortunately, they were quickly distracted. Ty and Katie peered through the screen door. "We just heard," Katie said as she moved to hug Laura. "I'm so sorry."

Ty added, "We came to help. What can we do?"

Laura tried to appear cheerful. "That's really sweet of you guys, but honestly, I don't know what more we can do. We told the police, so the sheriff is on the case. Or at least he's *supposed* to be." She rolled her eyes sarcastically.

Will recalled the sheriff's **lackadaisical** reaction. "Yeah, he didn't really inspire much confidence. In fact, he seemed more interested in accusing Dr. Perez of something than in finding him. He was giving Laura the third degree."

Katie thought that was standard police procedure, so that the sheriff could get a complete picture of what was going on.

Laura sighed loudly. "I just can't stand not knowing anything. I feel so helpless. I've already lost my mother, and now...."

The room fell quiet. Will felt terrible—he wanted to **abet** Laura and do something to help. "Why don't we look for him ourselves?" He glanced around expecting a **skeptical** response from his friends, but they thought it a **meritorious** idea. **Emboldened** by their interest, "We could retrace his steps—you know, figure out where he was before he disappeared. Maybe somebody saw something."

Laura was moved by her friends' enthusiasm. At least they were trying to stay optimistic. The four proceeded to reconstruct Dr. Perez's routine that day, and when Laura noted that her father had been spending a lot of time at the Historical Society, they all piled into Ty's car and drove over.

Daniel Bell greeted the foursome when they arrived. "The last time I saw your father?" He scratched his head. "I think it was at the town meeting the other night. But before then, he came here a lot to study." He led them into the records room, originally a dining room where the estate's guards ate. The former **refectory** was now a study, where important documents were exhibited.

"What was Dr. Perez doing here?" Will tried to ask politely, mindful of Bell's **choleric** attitude. He recalled the irritable tone Bell had used with students at school assemblies.

"He was looking at these," Bell pointed to several papers underneath the display case—yellowed newspaper clippings about the Titanic, a copy of McAllister's ticket, and McAllister's **patent** for his steam engine manufacturing process. "But he was especially interested in the will. Did you know that my great-grandfather, Clayton Bell, drafted the **writ** for McAllister? He was Algernon's personal secretary." He nodded at a pewter urn on a shelf that contained his relative's ashes.

"Really?" Will maintained his **civility**, despite Bell's **unwarranted** boast. After all, nearly everyone in town had an ancestor who served McAllister. "Do you mind if we just look around?"

Welcoming the friends to roam around, Bell extended his apologies to Laura. "I'm sorry to hear about your father. I've been enjoying my conversations with him so much. It's rare to find someone who **reveres** Red Fork's history as much as I do." He smiled before adding, "I look forward to many future discussions with him."

As soon as Bell left, Will **deployed** his friends across the chamber. Ty and Katie began rifling through the second floor file cabinets, while Will and Laura explored the rest of the collection: original estate deeds, a coffee-stained work order for marble, a cabinet filled with fine china, walls lined with black-and-white photographs and tapestries. The collection was nearly **impeccable** but, as Will noted to himself, curiously **devoid** of any mention that McAllister had been a "robber baron."

Laura stopped in front of a sketch of Stone Manor. It was a pretty picture set in springtime, with wild flowers along the lawn and birds feeding their young. After spending a minute taking it in, she looked to see the artist's signature: Will Lassiter.

Amazed at the **disparity** between this drawing and Will's other, darker portrayals, Laura was caught off guard. This one seemed too cheerful for him to have done. Before she could **chastise** him for the dishonest **portrayal**, Will sighed in embarrassment. "I know, I know. I don't believe the place embodies that kind of spirit either, but I had to do it for a school project and ... Anyway, that's why I gave it to Bell. It's more how he sees it."

The next image on the wall proved more intriguing. It was Will's great grandfather, in a photo nearly a century old. He was with an army of servants, dressed in crisp black and white, next to a horse and buggy in front of the manor. Analyzing the boyish face in the snapshot, Laura noted a definite resemblance between Will and Henry Lassiter.

Ty and Katie were also able to single out ancestors in the picture. Though the staff numbered well over 100, the servants all had the same **dour** expression and **stilted** formality. Under the photograph, a caption read, "Stone Manor—1908," and beneath that, a **pithy** comment: "Algernon McAllister provided a living condition for his staff that was extremely generous, especially given the **mores** of the time."

"What's that supposed to mean?" asked Laura.

"It means McAllister's servants were a *little* better off than those who worked for other **affluent** dudes," Katie remarked in a **droll** tone.

Ty **conceded** they hadn't found much of interest upstairs. "Some storage, an office, … and a closetful of red suspenders!" Ty's quip about Bell's **proclivity** for the support bands was met with only half-hearted grins.

As they made their way to leave, they passed a portrait of McAllister. Though it was hardly a new sight for Will, it caught his attention in a **novel** way. The sharp lines of the cheeks, the beady eyes with their dark pupils. Will stumbled as he turned away from the painting and caught up with his friends in the parking lot.

They rode home in silence, Laura quiet and **listless**. That changed when she saw that the note she'd taped on the front door for her father was no longer there. Thinking the best, she ran onto the porch, only to discover that the **missive** had just fallen from the door.

Their options had been **exhausted**, and the friends were **rife** with disappointment and anxiety. In their preoccupation with Dr. Perez's disappearance, they went back to Will's house and without pause, wolfed down Ken's latest offering. By the end of their meal, Laura was still **distraught**. "I'm never going to see him again, am I?" The possibility of finding her father was so **tenuous** by now that she thought he was dead.

Ken tried to be supportive. "Don't say that. It'll do no good to think the worst right now." His **dispassionate** words and **stolid** tone offered her little **solace**.

* * *

Will **parried** the first punch, but a second swing landed squarely on his jaw. He fell back, grabbing the coattail of his **nemesis** and pulling him into a beam of light. This time, Will saw the man's face and recognized him instantly. The black eyes and bony nose could only belong to Algernon McAllister.

McAllister **glowered** at Will for a moment and then, with a bloodcurdling roar, launched another attack. But this time Will was prepared. He struck out with such ease and ferocity that he knocked McAllister on his back.

McAllister struggled to regain his footing, though as he did, something else was **diverting** his attention: A woman was lying in the corner of the room. Her long brown hair covered her face, but Will knew who it was. "Laura!"

* * *

"Will!"

He opened his eyes and Laura stood over him. He blinked, unsure of whether he was still dreaming. He reached out and touched her with **ardor**. She was real.

It was three in the morning, and Laura couldn't sleep. "I started flipping through my father's journal." She held up the small book and **proclaimed** with **animation**, "I think we've got a lead!"

CHAPTER SIXTEEN

31 May

It's been seven years since Ellie died. It feels like a lifetime. I still remember our first date as if it were yesterday. What was the name of that little Thai restaurant off-campus? We talked so much, they kicked us out to close up. The food was terrible, but it didn't matter. Although it was springtime, the temperature had dropped to freezing. Ellie was shivering the whole night.

And then when she got cancer years later, her **extremities** were always cold. All the blankets in the house couldn't warm her. Laura was so young—I wonder how much she remembers. How different our lives would be if Ellie were here…I'm sure we'd still be in Phoenix. Certainly, we wouldn't have moved all over the globe, nor would I have ever heard of

Red Fork. But now I've dedicated my life to this project. I must know.

Laura reminds me more and more of Ellie every day. They're so much alike. Both with the same easy laugh, the same light in their eyes, the same self-assurance and courage. It's like Ellie is still here with me.

3 June

I told Laura about the move today. She's clearly unhappy, but as she always tries to be so supportive, she acted like it was no big deal. I feel bad—she was just starting to **adapt** to life here in Chicago. I have no idea how long we'll be **ensconced** in Red Fork, and whether we'll need to go somewhere else to continue the research. In the end, I hope she understands why I've done all this. And that she forgives me for her **nomadic** upbringing.

I think the trail is going to end with Stone Manor. Everything indicates that this is where it started. McAllister's such an **enigma**. For every fact I find, there's another one to challenge it. What was he hiding behind his guise as a generous **benefactor**? Was he really a **ruthless** businessman? I hope the answers are in Red Fork. Not sure what this will uncover.

14 June

McAllister Timeline:

1865: Born in Topeka, Kansas.

1879: Started his first business, transporting people via carriage from Abilene to Topeka.

1881: Bought a fleet of carriages & **augmented** route to St. Louis.

1887: Sold company and used profit to buy controlling interest in a small manufacturing plant in Pittsburgh.

1890: Plant produced state-of-the-art steam engines for locomotives and ships. Had stiff competition, but within a year he'd bought out two of his three rivals (most likely, **coerced** them into selling). Soon after, the third competitor lost everything in a mysterious fire. (Sabotage? Very possible, but authorities didn't investigate??)

1891: McAllister was the primary **donor** for the Pittsburgh mayor's successful re-election campaign. He obtained political **clout** and used it to alter local labor laws in his favor.

1892: Accused in Pittsburgh Gazette of being a **despot**. Reporter **editorialized** about horrendous working conditions in McAllister's plants. **Cited** one story about a worker losing his arm in a machine. The foreman halted all work to attend to the injury. McAllister was so **incensed** by the delay in production that he fired the foreman and docked every worker's pay that week—even though their salaries were already a mere **pittance**. McAllister sued reporter for libel and won, then bought Pittsburgh Gazette and fired said reporter.

1894: Now a multimillionaire, started **purporting** that he went to Harvard (no record of him ever being there).

1896: Purchased 1,000 acres outside of Pittsburgh and had Red Fork built.

1902: Moved into Stone Manor.

1909: Became **reclusive** and remained **cloistered** in Red Fork for the most part (?) Business started to fail, shrinking net worth considerably.

1910: His last public appearance.

1912: Died on Titanic, leaving land to servants in will. Remainder of fortune funded endowment of McAllister College.

16 June

I don't understand his will. It's like a king **abdicating** his throne. Why would he give it all to his servants? It's **farcical** to think that he treated them better than the workers in his plants. Maybe he had a change of heart? Who else was he going to give it to? He had no heirs. But why not? Why didn't he marry?

20 June

McAllister = orphan?

22 June

Our first night in Stone Manor. I can't sleep. There's so much to do. Need to **refurbish** the house—the wiring is ancient, the plumbing is even older, and there's a **grimy** film all over everything. But I can still picture what it must have been like in its heyday. McAllister entertaining guests in the ballroom. I grew up in a two-room apartment in Tucson, and now I'm living in a **palatial** mansion.

Something's strange about this place. Maybe it's the creaky floorboards or the fact it's so big, but I feel very uncomfortable here. Laura's trying hard to **adapt**; there's a boy next door who's about her age, so perhaps that will help. The town seems like a better place for her to grow up than Chicago.

25 June

The Titanic **paradox**, again. McAllister bought a ticket on the boat, but the passenger manifest doesn't list him as being aboard when it went down. And why would he, after two years of **seclusion** at Red Fork, suddenly decide to go to Europe? Perhaps the **axiom** "Rich people are just different" is correct. I wonder if the **symposium** about his legacy next month will address this. (Remember to RSVP.)

27 June

The so-called 'Curse of Stone Manor' is a fascinating example of suburban legend. Some believe that the deaths of Johnny Gunn and Helena Ross are somehow related to McAllister's death. I can't believe no one has stepped forward to **debunk** this myth. Gunn was a crook who skirted dangerous situations. The law of averages merely caught up with him, and he died while committing another crime. Simple as that. As for Helena Ross, she was already old and an invalid when she got here. It stands to reason she was on her last legs...so to speak.

Then there are the "unexplained" disappearances. I think Will Lassiter's theory is sound—it's probably just a story to scare kids. Two children did disappear in the early 60s, and the last eyewitness report had them playing near the manor. But, it's much more likely that they went down to the river and were swept away by the current.

I like Will. He's an **astute** young man, and Laura's enjoying his company. But it's clear he's scared of something here. He tries to hide it, but his behavior borders on **phobia**. I'm curious to find out more about that, and why he feels that way.

The Ring of McAllister? Ask D. Bell.

30 June

Bell confirmed Will's story about the ring, but he was really edgy about it. He was too quick to agree with me when I suggested it was at the bottom of the ocean. It was as though he knew that wasn't true. Of course, maybe I made a mistake bringing up the subject at all. Bell definitely knows more than he's letting on. I'll have to be careful around him. He won't understand why I'm doing this.

2 July

How did Gunn turn Red Fork into a massive brewing facility without anyone noticing?! He would have had to move the booze from the manor to the coal storage and then to the boathouse, without being spotted. Virtually impossible—perhaps he was '**compensating**' the local law enforcement for turning a blind eye?

An odd thing happened today: I was outside the house and I heard Laura scream. But when I ran inside, she said she was fine. She looked terrified. But when I pressed her for details, she shrugged me off. She's too self-sufficient...I wish she opened up to me more.

3 July

Research at Historical Society again. Came across an interesting interview McAllister gave with the Pittsburgh Gazette right after he built Stone Manor. He said he'd intended Red Fork as "a **sanctuary** for his children and children's children." So he planned on having a family after all! Then what's the deal with his will? Or did he consider his servants his children, as a **metaphor** of sorts? That's a creepy thought.

4 July

Anna Krause?

5 July

First the fire at Sal's and now the boathouse explosion. Both buildings were part of the original estate, and both were **integral** to Johnny Gunn's bootlegging operation. What's the connection?

The town meeting was unbearable…all those **cynics**. I feel terrible that Laura had to experience it. The best thing would probably be for us to stay home for the next few days, though if this mansion is a ticking bomb, who knows what could happen.

Speaking of this mansion…I would have thought it **inconceivable**, but I'm starting to believe there's a **latent** force in here—some sort of **entity**. Laura's **mishaps** are increasing, in number and severity. She fell again, and to hear her describe it, something pushed her. Laura is a graceful girl, I can't believe she's that clumsy. I have this **innate** feeling that she's in danger here.

*   *   *

"That's the last entry." Laura flipped the book closed. "The day he disappeared." She leaned back into the couch, dazed by her father's revelations. "The spirit my dad wrote about…" she murmured **furtively**, "You don't think he was talking about—"

"A ghost?" Will nodded grimly. The journal **corroborated** what Will had long suspected. "I wanted to tell you this before," he began, "but I kept getting sidetracked. But now, especially considering your father's **approbation**, I think you should know. It's about how I got this scar on my arm. It was more intense than how I first described it."

Will told Laura about how he had gotten lost in the manor years ago. "It was really ... a confusing and **harrowing** experience. There were things that happened that I still can't explain— especially the fact that something grabbed me on my way out. I have a feeling it was the same thing that pushed you down the stairs ... and choked you." He looked squarely at Laura, "I think it was McAllister's spirit. It's becoming pretty obvious that he's not the good guy we all thought he was."

The enormity of this statement hit Laura hard. She stared at Will for a long time, digesting his story. "The last place I saw my dad was in the house. Maybe *it* got him because he was trying to protect me!"

Will put his arm around a **tremulous** Laura, and **somnolently**, they snuggled deep into the cushions. Stone Manor threw its sinister shadow over the Lassiter house.

CHAPTER SEVENTEEN

*   *   *

A door was **ajar** at the end of the hallway, and Will looked in. There was Laura, in an intense struggle with McAllister. She was trying to get around him, to reach something he was shielding, but McAllister was too strong. He slapped her forcefully, pushing her back. **Impotent** to open the massive door, Will had no choice but to watch. He heard a baby crying in the background. Helpless, he was **immobile** with fear.

At one point, Laura turned and stared in his direction. He could see the urgency in her blue eyes. Blue eyes? Will squinted. *Laura doesn't have blue eyes.* And this woman looked a bit older, perhaps in her late twenties. Though she had the same long brown hair and **comeliness** as Laura, this was someone else. She seemed so familiar.

*   *   *

Will's heart was pounding. Outside, a dog was barking at the garbage men on their **diurnal** trek through the neighborhood. Will glanced down at Laura, sleeping soundly against his shoulder. He needed to splash cold water on his face.

He stuck his head under the faucet and slurped water into his mouth, but couldn't stop thinking about his dreams. *The same characters, the same setting. They must all be related.*

He decided to try sketching what he had seen: the dark corridor, the abusive McAllister, and the innocent woman. Struck by her **pulchritude,** he lingered for a while on the woman's face, and as he drew her **caricature,** he began to alter her expression. He changed it from the anguish he had seen in his dream to a more **doleful** look, a sadness brought on by a hard life. He'd seen this face before, and after a moment's concentration, he snapped his fingers: This was one of the servants in the photograph he'd seen at the Historical Society.

Laura was just getting up. She'd finally had a decent night's sleep. But before he came clean about his nightmares, Will wanted to confirm the woman's identity. **Adumbrating** his plan, he offered, "I want to go back to the Historical Society, to look at a photo again. It's probably nothing. But something jarred my memory."

His **cryptic** statement went unchallenged. Laura agreed, though she wanted to use the time to check on the sheriff's progress. They arranged to meet at Sal's afterward.

Daniel Bell was nowhere to be found at the Historical Society. Going straight to the photograph, Will scanned the row of maids, and fixed his eyes on one face. Though the image was faded by time, she was the woman in his dream: Anna Krause. *That's the name Dr. Perez jotted in his journal.*

Bell suddenly appeared, and Will whirled around. "Oh hi, Mr. Bell. Do you by any chance know who this is?" He pointed to Anna.

Donning his reading glasses, Bell moved closer. Squinting down his nose, he studied her face.

"Her name's Anna Krause," Will added, hoping to **expedite** the response.

"Krause? I don't recall there being much documentation about her." Bell left the room and returned with an old ledger. "Here we go. She left Red Fork about a year after this photo was taken. No forwarding address." He closed the book before Will could see what else was written and, folding his arms, pressed the **dilapidated** volume to his chest. "I'm afraid that's all there is. May I ask the reason for your sudden fascination?"

Will hadn't told Laura about his dreams, so he certainly wasn't going to tell Bell. He shrugged his shoulders openly. "It's kind of embarrassing. I noticed her yesterday and, well, I thought she was pretty. But I couldn't say anything with Laura around. Know what I mean?"

Bell's uneasy expression gave way to a smile. "Exactly! You may find this hard to believe, but I was once your age." He leaned in closer. "Your secret's safe with me." And with that, he practically pushed Will out the door.

Over at the pizzeria, the two friends hooked up, though Laura, too, had little news to share. "Well, they **canvassed** the town and alerted the state police, but they have no clues. And they still think my father and I had something to do with the explosions. I got the third degree from the sheriff all over again." She chewed on a mouthful of ice. "What about you? Did you find what you were looking for?"

Will studied the wet circles made by his glass. "I don't know. I found out who Anna Krause is. Or was. She was a maid at Stone Manor during McAllister's time."

Laura looked puzzled. "How did you—"

"Think to go to the Historical Society?" Will finished her thought. "Actually, I dreamt about her last night." At Laura's **incredulous** look, he shook his head. "I know … it's bizarre. I've been dreaming a lot lately. Nightmares mostly. I'm in the manor, I hear a woman yelling and a baby crying, and then I see McAllister. He's fighting with Anna Krause … or sometimes with me—and that's when I get this." He lifted his disfigured arm. "At first it didn't occur to me that the dreams were all connected. But this morning, I realized they're all different parts of one big scene.

They're trying to tell me something. I'm sure of it. Only I don't know *what* yet."

"How long have you been having these dreams?"

"Actually, they started the night you moved here...." Not wanting to sound accusatory, Will let his voice trail off casually. Now more than ever, Laura needed an ally, a friend she could lean on, and he didn't want to **kindle** any resentment. His mind raced through these **machinations**.

Laura hadn't taken offense. "It's probably just a coincidence. Look, you saw the name Anna Krause in my father's journal, and then subconsciously associated it with the photograph. Voilà, you dreamt about her. And since we also know from my dad's journal that McAllister was a creep, that's why you imagined him as the enemy."

While this **scenario** sounded **credible**, Will was sure that Laura wasn't convinced. But why she didn't say so puzzled him. "Do you really think that's all it is?"

"I don't know." Laura sat back and **deliberated** over her words. "It does sound pretty weird. Under normal circumstances, my **inclination** would be to think you mashed all these different things together in some **subliminal** way. But we're in a really bizarre **predicament**. In your dreams, McAllister is beating Anna Krause, and in real life, you and I are getting attacked by his ghost. It's all so unreal." Laura rested her head against the window, clearly exhausted. It was getting harder to distinguish fact from

hyperbole. "I don't know if learning more about Anna Krause will get us closer to finding my father. But he *was* interested in her— he had a question mark next to her name—and we don't have any other leads."

After lunch, they walked back to Town Hall and down to the Records Room. Every birth and death in Red Fork was **chronicled** there, not to mention all the property owners in town. Will asked the clerk, a short **dotard** named Mrs. Denton, for any and all information about Anna Krause. "She lived here about a hundred years ago," he offered.

Mrs. Denton **obligingly** made her way toward the back of the room. Kicking a stepladder into place, she climbed it slowly. The woman was obviously 10 years past retirement, but no one had bothered to tell her. "Did you say Claus?" Will **enunciated** the name again. At last Mrs. Denton called down. "I don't see anything here about any Krause." She descended the ladder in the same **precarious** manner as she'd gone up. "I'm sorry, dear."

Another dead end. Will and Laura let out a collective sigh and then, on a whim, asked if they could look around themselves.

"I'm not supposed to let anyone unauthorized back here." She eyed Will and Laura suspiciously, but detecting no trace of **malice,** was moved to compassion. "But what are they going to do? *Fire* me?" She lifted the counter and let them pass through. "Who was this Krause person? Maybe we didn't look in the right place."

Will explained that she had been a maid at Stone Manor.

"Krause? I don't know anyone in town with that name. Does she have any descendants here?" Mrs. Denton asked, walking down a row with books on either side.

"I don't think so," Will answered as he and Laura followed behind.

"Well, all the servants had to provide their personal histories to be considered for employment, even before Red Fork's **inception**." Mrs. Denton searched a stack of books with an unsteady hand. "Ah," she said, pulling a **tattered** volume from the shelf, "Here it is. Why don't you take a look at this while I take my lunch break?" She settled into an old recliner in another part of the room and flicked on a small TV. "Don't mind me," she called, "it's time for my favorite soap opera."

Will and Laura excitedly opened the book. They **pored** over the volume carefully, hunting the name Anna Krause. Will found several references to Lassiter, Martin, and Bell, along with practically everyone else he knew in town, but there was no Krause.

Will couldn't understand why Anna would have left Red Fork. No other worker under McAllister had left, and for good reason; their lack of societal status in those days would have **ascribed** them an impoverished life. Even if McAllister wasn't as **beneficent** and humane as they'd thought, serving him was surely better than living on the street. Will reconsidered, though, when he remembered the **nefarious** man in his dreams. *Perhaps being* ***destitute*** *actually was preferable to working for him.*

"This is so frustrating," Laura said as she slammed the book shut. She yelled out to no one in particular, "Who was Anna Krause?!"

"Sauerkraut?" Mrs. Denton called from the back. "No thank you, dear. Gives me gas!"

Despite their disappointment, Will and Laura had to laugh at the mix-up. They waved good-bye to the **amiable** clerk and headed out of Town Hall. There was nowhere to go but home.

CHAPTER EIGHTEEN

*　*　*

He couldn't see a thing, but Will could hear the **shrill** cry of a baby and the shuffling of feet. Then, a loud thud. The darkness that **beclouded** him gave way to light, and he found himself in a small room, standing near a fireplace. A vase rested on the mantle, its glass panels **refracting** the iridescent glow. The glossy mahogany walls shone. This could only be in Stone Manor.

The baby's wailing continued, but still, there was no infant to be found. Instead, a body lay **prostrate** on the floor. Long brown hair caught Will's eye. Anna! He bent down to turn over the body, but in fact, it wasn't the maid at all. It was Algernon McAllister.

McAllister had been bludgeoned to death, his bloody skull partially caved in by a heavy object. The sinister sneer on his face still remained, in **juxtaposition** to his own ghastly demise. Uneasy, Will felt a twinge of **compunction** as he leaned nearer to examine the body.

Blood started to **congeal** on Will's hands. It was sticky, and he was eager to wipe it off. As he stood up, his reflection in the mirror caught his eye—only it wasn't his own likeness staring back at him. It was that of an older man—a **disheveled**, grief-stricken face smeared with blood. Henry Lassiter!

Will gasped in shock, then noticed another motionless figure. It was the limp form of Anna Krause on the far side of the room, her neck twisted and her head **askew**. He knelt down beside her lifeless body, lifting her head into his lap. Immense sorrow gripped Will, and strangely, he was overcome with a feeling of intense devotion. He opened his mouth to speak, but another man's voice came out—that of his great-grandfather. "Anna!"

Seeing shadows, Will realized he was no longer alone. Ty, Katie, Ken, Joanne, and all the other residents of Red Fork had formed a ring around him, panic in their faces. He looked down at Anna again, but this time, he was outside the manor, holding a dirt-filled shovel. Oddly, the night's sky was **devoid** of stars, and he could barely see past the glow of a few lanterns. He desperately scanned the faces around him to find Laura and her father, but they were not among the crowd.

His **compatriots** wore an almost childlike expression, their faces begging to know who would care for them now. They looked to Will not for an answer but for recognition, some sort of acknowledgment and understanding.

But Will could offer no such **empathy**. He was busy burrowing a hole for these bodies. He pierced the earth forcefully with the handle. Daniel Bell nearby, supervising the excavation, tried to soothe Will's **aggrieved** state. "This has to be," he told Will.

*   *   *

Will awoke, wiped the perspiration from his forehead, and set about tackling what had now become his morning ritual— **extricating** himself from his twisted blanket. The imagery of the nightmare remained fresh in his mind, as he replayed the events. Did he just witness something real? Had his great-grandfather committed a **heinous** act? This was no mere **peccadillo**; it appeared that Henry had murdered Algernon McAllister. And, quite possibly, Anna Krause as well.

His great-grandfather's grief gushed through Will's veins. It was all a terrible mistake, he realized. Henry had tried to **deter** any aggression, but unfortunately his actions went **awry**, and they met with terminal results.

Gradually, Will regained his composure, though his **sensibilities** suddenly became heightened. As he sat up in bed, even the smallest sounds became **amplified**: a dog bark a mile away, a cricket outside, the ticking of the clock in the hallway downstairs. Swinging his legs to the floor, he concentrated on the **phenomenon**, and slowly, those sounds were **quelled** by a different sensation altogether. He couldn't put his finger on it at first; the **arbitrary** noises just faded away and there was silence. But **intermittently**, Will felt connected to the others in Red Fork, almost as a sixth sense. His desire to leave home and see the world suddenly seemed **frivolous** and ill-conceived. He sensed that he finally *belonged*.

This experience of **solidarity** was not a happy affair. Instead of feeling united with his neighbors, Will was initiated into a collective pool of guilt, and he felt **unadulterated** remorse. But before he could make sense of it, the sensation passed.

Will stood dumbfounded in the middle of his room, his mind racing. He rushed to his desk to document this experience on paper, but, struck by an afterthought, stopped in midsentence, tore out the page, and crumpled it up.

CHAPTER NINETEEN

Will tossed and turned for hours before drifting into a **restive** sleep, and by the time he awoke the next day, the sun was already high. He hobbled down the stairs to check on Laura, but when he walked into the den, she was absent from the room. Her sheets and blankets were piled in an unruly heap, and the curtains were still drawn.

Yanking open the garage door, he found his mother standing in the alcove she **appropriated** as an artist's studio and staring at her easel. "Mom, have you seen Laura?"

Startled by the **incursion**, Joanne looked up from her canvas, but her face relaxed into a smile when she saw her son. "Good morning, dear. No, I haven't." She turned back to her artwork, mixing colors on her **palette**, and said, "I left some French toast warming in the oven for you two."

But there was no time for breakfast. Will knew Laura was up to something, and he ran next door. A **recurring** noise of metal cutting into dirt led Will to the rear of the mansion, and there, beyond **serpentine** gravel paths that had once decorated the area, he found Laura. She was digging a hole.

Laura dug with purpose, strewing her large shovelfuls of earth around the lawn. She was so focused that she didn't see Will approach, and when she did, she spun to face him **wielding** her shovel like a weapon.

"Whoa!" Will fell back and shot his hands up to shield his face. "It's only me!" Laura gasped and blushed, embarrassed at her **impetuous** reaction.

Laura had woken up with an **impulse** to dig. And by this hour of the day, she had made a fairly large hole. Given his recent nightmare, this struck Will as oddly coincidental. *The only difference is, in my dream, I was the one doing the digging.* Not knowing what else to do, he grabbed another shovel and joined Laura in the hole.

With a **fervor** bordering on fanaticism, they worked for over an hour, scooping out soil and rocks. The sun beat down on them fiercely, but their pace didn't slow, and the **concave** opening soon became so deep that they stood eye-level with the ground. When that was done, Laura plunged in with her bare hands.

Whatever **spawned** this initiative remained mysterious to Will and, he suspected, to Laura too. Their efforts soon paid off, though, when they unearthed a smooth white object. Loosening the surrounding dirt, Will was able to push his hand beneath the **protrusion** and pull it out. He was looking at a human skull.

Promptly dropping the skull, Will jumped from the **morbid** sight. The two teens were paralyzed by their discovery. It was clear the head had been decapitated, and the cranium fractured along the right temple. Will recalled McAllister's fatal injury in his dream, and started to draw conclusions. "It's—"

Laura cut him off before he could finish: She had found another bone. That meant there were probably more bones below. In the end, they **exhumed** two skeletons that Will could identify, from remembering the illustrations in his anatomy book, as male and female. "But who are they?" Laura wondered.

"McAllister and Anna Krause," Will replied, no **vestige** of doubt in his tone.

Laura needed to know more. And Will was about to tell her, until he realized he'd also have to unmask his great grandfather's **iniquity**. And for that, he wasn't prepared. Instead, he pointed to the shiny metal mass on the jawbone. "A gold tooth. It has to be him. Who else could have afforded that?" He looked down at the soil on his palms and was reminded of the blood on Henry Lassiter's hands.

"And Anna? How do you know it's her?"

Will insisted **obdurately**, "It just is."

"Another dream?"

Before he could respond, Laura gasped. He followed her eyes down to the floor of the crater and saw murky water welling up from the bottom. Their feet were already submerged in thick mud, and the skeletons were disappearing quickly.

The two friends had no choice but to jump out. They quickly struggled against the **declivity** of the hole, watching the earth disintegrate beneath them.

"No!" A **rash** Laura tried to **retrieve** the disappearing skeletons, but Will restrained her. She struggled to **extricate** herself from his grip at first, but her energy soon depleted. Remaining in **stasis**, they watched as the hole filled to the brim with water.

The whole thing was over in seconds, their discovery gone. This wasn't a complete fiasco, though. A new mystery had been uncovered—one that was supported by Perez's journal and by Will's dreams. They could definitively **dispel** the myth that McAllister had died on the Titanic. The problem was, they were no closer to finding Laura's father. Or to understanding Will's nightmares.

Home and a hot shower beckoned the two friends. It was a much needed relief and helped pacify them both. They considered their next move.

"We have to tell somebody," Will said, drenching his French toast with syrup.

"But who? The sheriff? He'll think I murdered them or something." Laura's **glib** remark was understandable, given her run-in with Tompkins.

Ty and Katie arrived just in time for a little moral support. Though they tried to comfort Laura, they all knew that with every passing day, the likelihood of Dr. Perez's safe return diminished. Will and Laura stared glumly at their breakfast plates, while Katie nervously stirred her coffee. Finally, Ty broke the silence. "So what have you two been up to?"

Will held his tongue, unsure of how Ty and Katie would react to their find. But Laura had no such qualms. "We found a couple of skeletons buried in the back of Stone Manor."

"Oh my God!" Katie frowned in disgust. "Human skeletons? Could you tell who they were?"

"We think they're McAllister and Anna Krause."

Given Ty and Katie's blank expressions, Laura might as well have told them she'd found Elvis. "That's impossible!" Katie dismissed their theory with the **hackneyed** explanation, "How could it be McAllister? He was on the Titanic."

"No, he wasn't," Will explained. Remembering what Dr. Perez had told him, "There was no record of him ever boarding the ship."

"My father had the proof," added Laura. This momentarily stalled Katie, but she wasn't **daunted** for long. Acting in the role of prosecutor, she continued to challenge. "Even if that's true, and I'm not saying it is, how do you know it's McAllister?"

"His skull had a gold tooth."

"So?" Katie shrugged her shoulders. "That doesn't prove anything."

Will cleared his throat. "A hundred years ago, who else could have afforded gold teeth?" He knew this wasn't the most **cogent** argument, but he felt in his heart that it was true, and it was a belief he would **assert** with all his strength. He turned to Ty and **entreated** his friend to trust him. "It's McAllister. I can feel it." He rubbed his scar to emphasize his **clairvoyant** connection to the dead **magnate**.

Ty, recalling Will's childhood trauma, consented. "Okay, then let's see them." He gave Katie an assuring look. When neither Will nor Laura got up, Ty **reiterated**. "I mean we want to see the skeletons for ourselves."

Dejected, Will explained how the skeletons were gone, how they'd been swallowed by the water. He knew it sounded ludicrous. "One minute we were brushing the dirt off them, and the next minute all this water was rising up from the ground. We almost got stuck in there ourselves."

Not surprisingly, Katie and Ty had trouble believing this. Their first thought was to just go and dig up the yard again.

"We can't. The ground's too unstable over there, and I'm not willing to risk it." Will was becoming **querulous**. "If you want to see them so badly, you dig them up."

To keep the conversation from getting heated, Ty decided to change the subject. "So who was Anna Krause?"

"A maid at Stone Manor," Laura explained. "We came across her name in here," picking up her father's journal. "My dad was compiling information about McAllister and Red Fork, and he mentioned her." She pointed to the entry with Anna's name.

Ty had a harder time understanding just what Dr. Perez was referring to. "All he did was jot down her name. It's hard to know what he meant. Maybe we should go over this whole thing together. You know, you might have missed something."

Laura started to read the entries aloud. The first one spoke of her mother, and at this, she choked up. Putting his arm around her, Will assumed her place.

The first entries were tender and amusing, as Dr. Perez wrote of his wife and daughter. But the later ones were more shocking, in that they **demystified** the McAllister everyone knew. Not only did the entries **defile** his well-documented generosity, they also raised questions about his character.

Will reached the last entry and repeated the words **verbatim**, "I'm starting to believe there's a **latent** force in here—some sort of **entity**." Hearing the words aloud, he realized how **preposterous** this might sound to an **impartial** listener.

Not wanting to **instigate** another argument, Katie turned to Ty. "I think there's some interesting stuff in there. All **hypothetical** of course. But who knows what to make of it." She avoided eye contact with Laura. "Sorry."

Will now understood even more so than before how he was different from everyone else in Red Fork. He knew they'd have trouble accepting this news about McAllister's character. The

tenets of the town, after all, were based on his integrity and **benevolence**. Sure, the townspeople **lampooned** "Algernon" for his extravagances, but they'd never question, much less **denigrate**, his character. Why were they all **fettered** to such a narrow vision?

Frustrated, he slammed the journal closed, his thumb wedged in the crease of the book. He pulled it out and winced: a paper cut. *That's odd: My hand was on the middle of the page, not near an edge.* Reopening the book, he found the remnants of a page that had been neatly torn out—Perez's *actual* last entry. He scanned the blank page that followed it, and his eyes detected a single line of words that had been pressed into the paper from the previous listing.

"What is it?" asked Laura.

"Hand me that pencil," Will instructed.

With the instrument in hand, he angled it and started lightly shading the impressed area of the blank page. As he scratched at the paper, some words were revealed:

July 5, 1 pm   St Bartholomew's Orphanage

Laura recognized the date. "That's when he disappeared."

As her statement sunk in, the four friends considered what to do. Ever the **proponent** for law and order, Katie suggested they go to the police. Will, on the other hand, preferred an alternative. He was having visions of the **surly** sheriff.

"Let's check it out ourselves. It's our best lead yet. I have a good feeling about this."

CHAPTER TWENTY

Will knew of no orphanages in town, so he punched in "St. Bartholomew's" on the Internet. The results numbered well into the thousands.

"Just look for orphanages," Ty offered, chomping at the bit. Any ventures involving computers were his **forte**. He itched to take Will's place and navigate the mouse, but he **deferred** to his host.

Accepting Ty's **intimation**, Will keyed in the new variables. That, too, produced a **surfeit** of entries. "Any other bright ideas?" he asked.

"Change it so it's not a global search."

Will narrowed the search **parameters** to show orphanages only in Pennsylvania. He crossed his fingers and clicked. Success. A manageable list of 20 or so organizations came up.

His friends all leaned in. Nothing went by the name St. Bartholomew's, but Laura noted another entry: New Hope Home for Children.

"My father had an appointment at an orphanage, and the nearest one to Red Fork is this New Hope one. Is it possible it used to be called St. Bartholomew's? Search engines are a pretty recent innovation … maybe it's been renamed?"

Impulsively, Will picked up the phone and dialed the number on his screen. After a brief conversation with someone on the other end, he signaled a thumbs up. Indeed, the New Hope Home for Children used to be called St. Bartholomew's.

"Great! Then you're just the people I want to speak with. Do you keep an appointment book of your visitors? Could you tell me if an Octavio Perez visited you on July fifth?" He listened intently. "Well, do you know if he was coming to discuss anything specific? Okay, thanks." He placed the phone back in its cradle. Evidently, Perez had been scheduled to see the director but never showed up. That's all they knew.

"How about a little road trip?" Will enthused.

Ty **averted** his eyes. "I don't know. Granville's, like, a hundred miles away. It's all the way over in the next *county*." The way he expressed his doubt, Ty seemed to consider the two-hour drive an **arduous** trek into the **hinterland**.

Will was fuming. "What's the point of having a license if you don't want to go anywhere?"

"This isn't about that, Will," Ty said, becoming **agitated** himself. While he wanted to help, he wasn't sure whether his car could make the trip.

Will knew Ty well enough to know that he always kept his car fine-tuned and fully **operative**. But instead of challenging him, he dropped the subject. "Then maybe Ray can take us." Will hoped that by **invoking** his brother's name, it might stir Ty to action.

Unfortunately, Ty could see what Will was getting at. He smiled at his friend's **wily** attempt to persuade him. "Sorry, but Ray's at work."

Spurned yet again, Will pleaded one last time. "I'll pay for the gas. I'll buy you lunch. New tires. Whatever. Just take us there."

Ty looked to Katie. She, too, was **curt**. "Look, we don't want to go! Why do you have to keep pushing? And anyway, the sheriff's all over this. You think you're going to solve this all by yourselves? I don't mean to sound **apathetic** but someone has to be the voice of reason here. The truth is, there's nothing more we can do."

Will couldn't accept her logic, and he was baffled by his friends' **inexorable** stance. Visiting the orphanage could only help their cause. Was their **unyielding ethos** due to a fear of leaving Red Fork? Will **relished** the childhood days when he and Ty had more in common. *Come to think of it,* he realized, *Ty was infatuated with the idea of becoming an astronaut back then. I can't imagine a career that takes you farther away from town.* The more Will relived his acquaintance with Ty, the more he was convinced that his friend's **disinclination** to leave their **refuge** had grown increasingly stronger the older they got.

Still, Ty and Katie had raised an important point, a thought that Will and Laura had been **loath** to entertain: Maybe they really were ill-equipped to solve this mystery by themselves. Maybe the sheriff, despite his **pugnacious** manner, was far more capable of **ascertaining** the doctor's whereabouts.

Will weighed both possibilities, but ultimately **deferred** to his friend. "You know what, Ty? You're absolutely right." Despite Laura's puzzled look, he continued. "I guess we got a little crazy. The best thing would be to sit and wait."

"Thank you!" Katie exclaimed, relieved that Will's **quixotic** manner was finally giving way to sense. "I'm glad you're finally seeing the light."

"Me too," Laura added, finally in tune with Will's **ploy**.

The conversation then turned to the **mundane**, from DVD releases to the lack of rain. The **palaver** continued for more than an hour, and at a lull, Ty and Katie departed for home.

Will didn't begrudge his **benighted** friends, though he was clearly disappointed. It was, after all, a **sensibility** that was **indigenous** to the people of Red Fork. Why he was immune to it, he didn't know, but for the first time in his life, he was able to **divine** that his uniqueness here wasn't some stigma. If anything, it was a blessing, a gift that gave him the ability to see beyond the commonplace.

Hours later, when all was quiet and dark in the Lassiter household, an **invidious** series of beeps roused Will. He opened his eyes and silenced the alarm. It was 4:30 in the morning.

Dressing quietly, Will tiptoed by his parents' bedroom. He passed Laura, too, asleep in the den. **Gingerly**, he lifted a set of keys from the shelf and opened the front door, stepping out into the crisp morning air.

The first light of day was still more than an hour away, but already most of the stars had faded. Will walked to his mother's car and climbed in. He wanted to make sure no one awoke, so he put it in neutral, climbed out, and pushed it to the street. It was only once he reached Algernon Drive that he started the engine.

No sooner had Will gone 10 feet, than he slammed on the brakes. Laura was standing in his way, arms crossed **defiantly**. She ordered him out of the car.

Will resisted. "Go back to sleep. I just want to check something out."

"You can't drive without a license."

Her authoritative tone jarred him. Why was she being so **obstinate**? To him, it was an **inconsequential** point. "It's just a piece of paper."

"It may be. But I've seen you 'drive.'" She opened his door and ordered him to move over. "I already *have* my license," she boasted. Sliding the gear into drive, she steered the car down the street.

CHAPTER TWENTY-ONE

They rode in silence onto the interstate, preoccupied with the task at hand. They didn't even know what questions to ask at the orphanage. Would it truly lead them to Dr. Perez?

Verdant hills in the distance, Will couldn't help but take in the scenery. Green pastures extended as far as the eye could see, interrupted only occasionally by a tractor or ramshackle barn. The contrast between his own life and the **agrarian** life out here struck him. He was so sheltered in Red Fork. In fact, he'd never even been this far from home before.

They came upon a large group of cows grazing in a pasture. Opening his window, Will was abruptly greeted by their overpowering **bovine** scent. Foul odor filling the car, Laura broke the silence. "I hope that's not you."

Will smiled at the **ephemeral** waft. "I was going to ask you the same thing."

The herd stretched for more than a mile, and by the time Will and Laura reached the far end of the pack, they'd grown accustomed to the ripe smell. As they passed the last of the cattle, they could actually hear the animals **low** to one other.

The open land stretched out before them, and Will envisioned a new world ahead: New York, Chicago, and Washington D.C. nearby, and Canada, Mexico, and South America beyond. He wanted badly for Laura to keep driving—to leave his past behind and start a new life, out there. But her swollen eyes reminded him how much she needed his help. And that meant returning to Red Fork.

Laura detected his gaze. "A penny for your thoughts?"

"Just thinking about farming. What it would be like to be a farmer."

"You?" She laughed heartily. "I just got this image of you in overalls. Frightening." She **pondered** the idea of Will **husbanding** a strip of land. "Still, you'd create some pretty amazing artwork on fields like these. I'd love to see them."

An hour later, after cutting through a small town consisting of an old gas station and two **squalid** farms, they came upon a blue and yellow **logo**. New Hope Home for Children. Through two stone gates and up the driveway, they entered the compound, on which Will counted four buildings. The three within direct view were of a **utilitarian** design, simple rectangular structures that housed classrooms and a gym. The fourth was the one to dominate the otherwise **spartan** campus. Set off from the others, it was a large Victorian house with a wraparound porch and a **surplus** of gables.

They parked in front of the orphanage and stepped up onto the porch, only to find that the initially striking quality of the house **belied** its true condition: peeling paint, loose floorboards, and torn screens. A weathered wooden swing exposed the old age of the house; etched in the well-worn seatback was "St. Bartholomew's Orphanage."

Will knew little about orphanages and had only "seen" them in movies. From the outside, New Hope had met his cinematic **criterion**: cavernous **habitats** forgotten by time, with occupants who'd been **forsaken** by humanity; but once inside, his **pejorative** vision was **dispelled**.

Surprisingly clean, the facility seemed rather nurturing. The kids looked well-fed, even highly **engaged**, and with **prevalent** sunlight, the atmosphere was cheerful. Video games, jigsaw puzzles, and reading anthologies could be found around the room—not to mention piles of *National Geographic*, which Will **duly** noted.

With the squeak of Will's shoes on the newly mopped floor, they **inadvertently** announced their arrival. Skip, a short thirty-something with a close-cropped beard, greeted them. "How can I help you?"

"Um…." Will stuttered a bit before coming up with a believable answer. "I'm trying to draw my family tree for a reunion, and one of my great-grandparents was left here. I was hoping I could get some information."

Skip was enthusiastic in his response. "What a great project to take on. Good for you!" He swung around in his chair to face his computer and, after a few clicks of the mouse, turned back to Will. "What's the last name?"

Will and Laura were both caught off-guard. Will stared blankly, wracking his brain for a response. He was about to say his own last name when Laura blurted out "McAllister ... or Krause."

Skip raised his eyebrows as he typed in the names. "Most of these records are confidential, and the ones that aren't contain only the most **banal** facts. So I'm not sure there will be anything here that you don't already know." He studied the screen: There was nobody in the system under either name.

Dispirited, Will sighed. They'd come all this way for nothing? This **nadir** in their investigation left them more frustrated than ever. But just then, a lightbulb went off: "The baby would have been left here around 1910. Do the **natal** records go that far back?" *Just because the files aren't in his computer*, Will reasoned, *it doesn't mean they don't exist.*

Sure enough, Skip's face lit up. While the computer files went back to the thirties, there was paper documentation earlier than that. The suddenly **efficacious** Skip led them down to the basement, and into a large storage room. "Geez, this is an **archaic** filing system. I tell you, computers make things *so* much easier." Going straight for a particular shelf, he pulled down an archival box dated January–June 1912, and from that, a thick brown book. He handed it to Will.

Will flipped through the book, eager for a clue. And when he got to March 5, 1912, it didn't disappoint: A baby girl, Elizabeth, had been left at St. Bart's on that date. The **transcription** jumped out at him. *Familiar, but how?*

Finally, his face lit up. "March 5, 1912. That was the day McAllister left for Europe. And he was supposed to return on the Titanic a month later." But he and Laura already knew McAllister wasn't on the boat and figured he'd never even made the trip. Will looked at the mother's name: A. Krause.

"Anna!" Laura whispered loudly into his ear. "Who was the father?"

Will ran his finger to the space listing the infant's **paternity.** It was blank, and, other than a pediatrician's signature certifying that the neonate was healthy, there was only one significant detail—a Chicago couple, Carole and Ben Brewster, had adopted her three days after her arrival at the orphanage.

Will had one last request—to get a photocopy of their discovery—which Skip was happy to **oblige.** Pleased with their success, Will and Laura paid their thanks to the gracious clerk and began their journey back home.

As the Victorian house **receded** into the background, Laura **exhorted** Will. "It's time you fessed up," she said with **equanimity.** "Tell me about your dreams."

"What are you talking about? I've already told you everything."

"No, I mean about the bodies we dug up. How were you so sure that they were McAllister and Anna Krause?"

Will had to **concede**. He described the nightmares in detail, from the vague wanderings in Stone Manor to the **vivid** details of his **altercation** with McAllister—to the repeated cries of an infant.

"That's got to be Elizabeth," Laura said. She wanted more details.

Will described the bodies he'd seen and the bizarre burial, though he felt **compelled** to omit his great-grandfather's role. Henry Lassiter's **culpability** still troubled Will, and he couldn't yet accept it as fact: How could he reconcile his ancestor's violent thoughts with the sorrow he'd felt in the final nightmare?

Laura listened to the **abridged** description and offered a verdict. "McAllister was Elizabeth's father. That makes the most sense. He probably had affairs with lots of his maids, and he must have gotten one of them pregnant."

The idea that McAllister was a **philanderer** wasn't earth shattering to Will. He'd come to understand that Red Fork's champion was anything but heroic. What he couldn't believe was that his great-grandfather would kill another man merely for being **amoral**. No, passion had propelled Henry Lassiter to commit this **heinous** act. But what was he passionate about? *Was it some sort of love triangle?* Will calculated the possibilities and came up with an unsettling theory—one that was at least equally **plausible** to Laura's idea: that *Henry* could have been baby Elizabeth's father, and he attacked McAllister for forcing himself onto Anna.

CHAPTER TWENTY-TWO

Driving home, Will tried to prepare himself for the tongue-lashing he was about to receive. At best, he'd be grounded for only a month, which wouldn't be so bad as long as it wasn't coupled with the "no TV" provision. Of course the other possibility was that he might be forbidden from driving a car again. He'd never get his license, which would mean he'd be forced to live his whole life in Red Fork. His dream to leave would become **obsolete**, and he'd be left to mow lawns.

Will longed to delay his return as long as possible. With a bit of wishful thinking, he wondered whether their discovery at the orphanage might **mitigate** his parents' anger, and in turn, **commute** his sentence.

"What should we do now?" Laura asked.

Will had been so busy **wallowing** in self-pity that he hadn't even considered their next course of action. Though he had no definitive plan as of yet, he felt under pressure to produce a **viable** suggestion. "Um, well, now that we know about the baby and Anna Krause and, since we don't want to go to the sheriff and I'd rather avoid my parents for the time being, maybe we should go talk to Mr. Bell." His **circumlocution** went over surprisingly well with Laura, and the plan was set.

Coasting back down through the rustic valley, the **reminiscent effluvia** of cows filled the car. This time, the smell was unbearable. Will wondered if the cows had simply eaten more grass or if the dung had baked in the **arid** afternoon. Laura, on the other hand, was **encumbered** by no such thoughts of **causality**—she gunned the engine, sending the car flying well past the speed limit. A good five miles later, they escaped the **malodorous** cloud.

They passed McAllister College, rode back into town, and pulled up to the Historical Society. Besides meeting Bell, they wanted to re-examine the photograph with Anna Krause in it. Walking up to the front porch, Will noticed for the first time the withering vines of ivy that ran up the side of the house. The leaves had turned brown, and the tendrils had started to curl out. *Death and decay ... how* **apt***.*

Much to Will and Laura's dismay, the display wall was bare. The photo had evidently been taken down.

Just then, Daniel Bell entered the room. Left thumb around his suspender, he joked, "I should give you your own set of keys!"

Laura adopted the courteous tone she'd seen Will employ with Bell. "We just came from the New Hope Home for Children. It used to be called St. Bartholomew's—" At her mention of the orphanage, Will thought he saw Bell's cheek twitch ... *or maybe it was just an eye tic.* "And my father was scheduled to do some research there but he disappeared before he had a chance. So, since we're trying to retrace his steps, we ended up going and found out that Anna Krause left a baby girl there. We think McAllister was the father." Laura paused **tentatively**, hoping Bell didn't think them **impertinent**. Nor did she want him to feel his authority **undermined**. Suddenly **obsequious**, she asked Bell his opinion.

Bell looked like a child whose **peer** had just told him Santa Claus wasn't real. The veins in his neck swelled out and his mouth moved rapidly, but no sound emerged. When he finally spoke, his voice was hollow and cold. "What proof do you have?"

Laura tried not to be **daunted** and focused instead on maintaining her **decorum**. "The baby was left on the same day that McAllister supposedly left for Europe."

"Supposedly?" Bell almost screamed. He gestured **animatedly** to a nearby display case. "His final trip is well-documented: ticket stubs, his itinerary. What right do you people have to come in here and—." He shook his head forcefully and tried to regain his composure. This was an **affront**.

"I understand that this is a stressful time for you, but to make these wild accusations that **sully** the immaculate reputation and very legacy of such a great man—all because a few dates happen to coincide. It's irresponsible and plain offensive. He would never have been mixed up in anything so **sordid**."

Laura stood her ground against his protestation. "But that's just it. My father's research showed that a lot of these stories about McAllister are just that—stories. How could he have been on the Titanic when he's buried in my backyard?"

"Buried in your backyard? You found a body?" Bell's eyes nearly popped out of his head. "Where is it now? And who else knows about this?"

"It sunk back into the ground, along with Anna Krause's skeleton," Will explained, taking Laura's arm and backing away from the red-faced historian.

Bell laughed pompously. "You have a lot to learn about research, young man. For starters, you must always be able to verify your claims."

Will resented this **complacent** attitude and wanted desperately to trip up Bell, to find a way of making the chunky fellow squirm. Suddenly, **excerpts** from Dr. Perez's journal flashed through his head, and one phrase stood out: 'The Ring of McAllister—Ask D. Bell.' *Why not just call it McAllister's ring?* He took a chance. "What do you know about the Ring of Mc....?"

"The Ring?" Bell turned white. "I suppose it's at the bottom of the Atlantic Ocean." He smirked and arched his back. "Speaking of which, that skeleton you said you found—if it was really McAllister, where was his ring?"

"Stolen," Laura theorized. "Probably by the man who killed him."

"No," Will mumbled to himself, "Henry didn't take it."

"What did you say?" Laura turned to him suddenly, and Will realized he'd actually verbalized his thoughts.

"In my dream, I didn't see a ring," Will admitted. Laura stared at him, and he went on. "No, I didn't tell you everything. I couldn't. But in my dream, I—or my great grandfather Henry— killed McAllister." He turned to Bell. "And you were there!"

Bell wasn't as surprised by the accusation as Will felt he should have been, considering it came from a nightmare. Instead, the **curator** leaned on the fireplace and looked straight into his accuser's eyes. "You'd be well advised to drop this matter."

This veiled threat only strengthened Will. "If I was Henry Lassiter in my dream, then maybe you were Clayton Bell. Why would your great-grandfather want to bury the bodies?"

Will didn't expect Bell to answer, much less react with the sudden outburst that followed. "You dolt!" Bell yelled as he lunged at Will with an iron poker. Will ducked to his left and fell back. His **agile** maneuver only enraged the normally **staid** historian further. "You've gone too far," he snarled. "You should have left it alone."

Backing away, Will stuck his hands out to show his defenselessness and struggled to speak in a soothing tone. "Now hold on a second! This is all just a big misunderstanding!"

"Yes it is, you selfish meddler," Bell roared back, taking another swing and missing. His attention—and **wrath**—focused fully on Will, Bell didn't see Laura snatch the urn, and as he dove at Will with **inimical** intent, she rushed up from behind and smashed the metal vase down his head. Bell dropped to the floor, the carpet covered in Clayton Bell's remains.

Within seconds, Will and Laura were out of the house. On the sidewalk, Will glanced back at the Historical Society, still dazed by what he'd just witnessed: the mild-mannered **pedant** he'd known his whole life, now a **pernicious** being, **deviated** from sanity. They watched Bell burst through the front door, a gray cloud of ash trailing him, and ran to their car. Peeling away from the curb, they left Bell—and a scorched set of tire marks—in their wake.

In his own car behind, Bell was right on their tail. Twisting around a corner, Laura veered into a parking lot near the lake, steering to halt behind some parked cars. As Bell entered the lot, Laura floored the gas pedal and zoomed past him back onto the street.

They sped north along the river, until they reached the upper end of town. When it seemed the chase would be **interminable**, Will thought it best to return to the business district. Fortunately, right on McAllister Boulevard, he spotted the sheriff. He had just come from the Red Fork Café.

Laura quickly pulled up next to Tompkins. "Sheriff! You have to help us. Daniel Bell is trying to kill us!"

Not surprisingly, Tompkins was unconvinced.

Will leaned around Laura to see the sheriff. "We told him that we found McAllister's skeleton at Stone Manor, and about the child he had with Anna Krause, and Bell just went nuts."

"A what—a skeleton?"

Will's voice conveyed his panic. "Look, he's almost here. Will you please help us?"

Tompkins leaned through the open window and addressed Laura. "Why don't you just calm down and give me the keys to your vehicle?" Laura was furious. Once again, the sheriff was treating her like the guilty party.

Bell was now coming over on foot. Will looked back at the sheriff, who was arguing with Laura, and realized that Tompkins was stalling. Stalling for Bell, that is. Will yanked Laura into the car.

Their car peeled away from Tompkins just as Bell had joined him. The **ignoble** pair stepped into the police car and followed with sirens blaring. "The Law" close behind, Laura buckled her seat belt with one swoop of her arm and sped down McAllister Boulevard, **evading** nearby cars and pedestrians.

With surprising skill, she executed a series of sharp turns from one side street to another. Eventually, it looked like they had lost the sheriff, though they knew they had to get out of the car fast. They made their way over to Will's house and parked.

Thinking they'd be better off hiding in Stone Manor, they ran over there, entering the **foreboding** structure without hesitation.

They watched the police car arrive at Will's house, Tompkins and Bell striding purposefully from the curb. Ken opened the door to greet them, then shook his head: He was pointing to Stone Manor.

"Nice going, Dad," Will pronounced as Tompkins and Bell started toward the manor. He quickly latched the dead bolt on the front door and guided Laura farther into the mansion. "Maybe they'll be too afraid of the ghost to come in," he said with stony **irony**.

Outside, Tompkins and Bell were trying to force open the door, and they weren't alone. Their backup had arrived. When the great oak slab wouldn't budge, Tompkins **resorted** to weaponry. He drew his revolver and fired two shots at the lock. The door creaked open.

In the end, Bell entered alone. Tompkins, along with his sidekicks, chose to wait outside, though they acted unfazed. Their **trepidation** about the house had seemingly kicked in.

Bell took a step inside, and out of earshot of his comrades, muttered, "Morons." With a **baleful** expression, he walked toward the stairs, getting within 10 feet of where Will and Laura were hiding. A creak turned him in the direction of the dining room.

Will tried to think quickly. He knew they'd have to disappear, and the basement seemed the ideal spot. Creeping down the staircase, they headed for the far end of the cellar. They navigated around boxes, furniture, and pillars, guided by **paltry** light, before finding the perfect **niche**, a mere six feet by three.

They could hear Bell's **lumbering** steps above them. The **curator** seemed to be walking around in a circle before **ascending** the stairs to the second floor. A few minutes later, Bell returned to the main level, evidently having found the basement door.

Will had locked the door behind him, and he now realized this was a dead giveaway. Why else would the door be locked from the inside, unless there was someone beneath to bolt it? Their **quandary** grew worse when Bell forced his considerable **girth** against the door and managed to shove it open. His steps echoed thunderously as he started down the stairs.

Will groped around for a possible weapon. His fingers closed around a metal handle, and he yanked on it thinking it was a shovel or a pick. It barely moved.

As if this wasn't enough to deal with, part of the wall suddenly gave way, pushing Laura and Will forward. They found themselves in an **adjacent** area that was cordoned off by a wall of thin wooden paneling. Peering through the slats, Will and Laura watched as Bell flicked on a light at the bottom of the staircase and began to scan the room. He noticed the alcove, stepped up to the wall, and squinted through the boards. Luckily, the room's **obscurity** was an effective shield, and Bell couldn't see much. He soon moved away, over to other openings in the room, and eventually back up the stairs. Will and Laura heaved a sigh of relief and took in their new surroundings. They'd found a secret chamber!

CHAPTER TWENTY-THREE

Though they had **eluded** Bell and were out of immediate danger, Will and Laura were reluctant to flee the mansion. Their pursuers might be waiting outside. Besides, they were intrigued by this previously unknown level of Stone Manor.

The room into which they'd fallen was little more than an antechamber, connecting the firewood compartment with a narrow corridor. Will groped overhead for a light, and the hallway became dimly illuminated. A handful of portable lamps hung from pipes along the ceiling, which, based on their depression-era design and rate of corrosion, Will guessed were at least 70 years old.

Next they came to some small bedrooms. Moths had eaten away at most of the intricate lace adorning the oak furniture, and thick dust **enshrouded** the interior. An unnatural stillness draped the rooms, though it was easy to appreciate how they had been

stylized to match the standards of Victorian high society. A valet's uniform hung from a door hook, suggesting it had been a servant's quarters.

Following the hallway around to the left, Laura was dumbstruck. "Wow, this is awesome. My dad never mentioned this place to me. Probably because he didn't know about it."

An iron strongbox caught their eye, and in it, stacks of fifty-dollar bills. "I bet no one's been down here since Johnny Gunn," Laura said, eyeing the cash. "This money's from the twenties," she pointed at the stamps indicating the year in which the bills had been minted. "And there's how he earned it." She nodded to a nearby box containing several unopened liquor bottles.

Leaving the money intact, they continued down the hallway. They stopped frequently, transported in time by the art. Beginning to recognize some of the paintings, Will couldn't help but predict aloud what they'd find around each corner. "I've been here before. In my dreams."

Laura wanted to know more. "What did you mean about being your great-grandfather in your dream and then killing McAllister?"

Will explained that was what happened, how he was standing over McAllister's body and covered in blood. "Anna's body was nearby. I don't know, maybe I killed her too. I didn't witness the actual murders, but I could feel—in my great-grandfather's body—that it was all a big mistake. I could feel it down to my bones. The next thing I knew, I was in the backyard burying the bodies while everyone watched." The words flowed as if they were a deathbed confession. It felt good to **divulge** and free himself of this **constraint**.

Laura had another take on Anna's murder. She thought Will's great-grandfather was trying to protect her from McAllister. "He probably killed her, and then your great-grandfather killed him. What if McAllister and Anna had a child, but he was embarrassed because Anna wasn't rich—"

"Maybe he was trying to kill the baby," Will cut in, advancing her theory a step further.

"Right! Because 'McAllister wouldn't be involved in anything so **sordid**,'" Laura mimicked Bell's nasal twang. "Maybe he was ashamed of his relationship with Anna, one of his servants, and wanted to **quash** the evidence—the baby he'd fathered. Anna tried to protect her child from him, and in doing so got herself killed."

Will shook his head. "Even if that's right, how does my great-grandfather end up killing McAllister, except maybe out of vengeance? I really don't think he was that kind of person."

"McAllister was too strong for her, he was just too strong. Henry tried to stop him, but in the end there was a terrible accident. Both Anna and McAllister were dead." She spoke with **conviction**. "That's why you felt such remorse in your dream."

"How can you be so sure?" Will snapped back. He was angry and frustrated, but as soon he'd spit the words at her, he regretted his **bellicose** tone.

Laura paused before she continued matter-of-factly, "You're not the only one who's been dreaming lately."

Will was stunned. He struggled to put together a **coherent** response. "But," he started, his voice cracking, "You said you hadn't dreamed since you moved into the manor."

"That's right. But the last few nights I've stayed at your house. And I've dreamt what you've dreamt. I'm sure of it: There was nothing more your great-grandfather could've done."

Will's head was still spinning when they came to the end of the hallway. A large door stood before them. He tried to open it, but the door wouldn't give. The wood was warped. Will planted his feet on the ground and leaned in, forcing the door open.

Bookcases overflowing with **tomes** took up three walls, and a large fireplace dominated the fourth. Will ran his hand along the mantle, feeling the coldness of the stone on his fingertips. The air was especially stale in here. He turned back to Laura, and in the faint light from the hallway, he saw the unmistakable likeness of Anna Krause. He knew exactly where he was. This was the room in his dreams.

Laura, too, could feel the significance of the room. There was an old **perambulator** in the corner, most likely the very carriage that held baby Elizabeth on that fateful night back in 1912.

McAllister had come in and demanded the child, but Anna wouldn't let him have her. She tried to fight him off but couldn't, as he was overpowering. Hearing Anna's screams, Henry rushed in to protect her, trying to come between her and her **nemesis**, but the robber-barron fended him off. Seeing Henry reel back from McAllister's blows, Anna charged at McAllister, but he grabbed her by the neck with his outstretched arm and began to choke her. She struggled against his tight grip but in vain. Her lifeless body dropped to the floor, hands falling to her side.

Henry lunged toward McAllister to **avenge** Anna's death, but McAllister, far larger in size, easily **deflected** his flailing punches. McAllister began pushing him toward the burning fireplace. The flames growing nearer, a desperate Henry curled his body around and reversed their positions. The twist created a momentum that swung McAllister directly into the mantle, his head smacking against the stone ledge. The blow to his skull killed him instantly.

Henry dropped to his knees. Shocked at having taken a life, his body went numb and he looked out in a daze. He wanted to repent the sin, but no one was there to forgive him.

Blinking rapidly to clear his head, Will snapped out of his trance. It was all just as Laura had described—a terrible accident. How could Laura have seen it with such **clarity**? This fully **exonerated** his great-grandfather from both deaths. Henry had killed McAllister in self-defense. But still, why did Henry bury their bodies in an unmarked grave? Could Laura **elucidate** this act as well?

A low rumble in the hallway stopped him from asking. The walls began to vibrate, knocking books and lamps from their perches. A sudden gust of wind blew into the room and rustled loose papers on the shelves. The **eddy** kicked up dust and grew stronger until it was a massive swirl of flying books and debris. Caught in the eye of this **maelstrom**, Will and Laura clung to one another to anchor themselves. The door slammed shut, cutting off the light from the corridor. In the pitch darkness, the vortex **dissipated**, and the two teens stood trembling in the center of the room.

A hissing sound much like that of a gas stove abruptly sang out around them, and the fireplace lit up. Will pressed Laura even closer, wishing now that they had chosen to stay in the basement and take their chances against Bell and Tompkins. The hiss grew into a growl, and a familiar voice, raspy and **malevolent**, whispered "Lassiter."

Will and Laura looked toward the sound and watched as a dark **amorphous** shape rose from the floor. Almost like a shadow thrown by the flames, it spread across the room toward them. It was the same silhouette that haunted Will in his nightmares—the **dormant** spirit of Algernon McAllister. Will pushed Laura behind him, and they both backed up toward the door.

Laura yanked on the doorknob with all her might, trying to **pry** the heavy door from its misshapen frame. As she pulled on the

recalcitrant handle, Will braced himself for contact with the spirit. The **nebulous** form passed over him, and he felt an **acute** pain shoot through his arm. The same **talon**like grip that had torn open his forearm all those years ago clasped at him again, and this time, its **virulent** hold was tighter, its cut deeper. The scar reopened and **hemorrhaged**, forcing Will to scream out in pain as he ripped his arm from the clutches of the shadow.

Fleeing into the corridor, they tried to retrace their steps. The walls shook on either side of them, and McAllister's maniacal laugh echoed in their ears as they turned left, then right. Rounding a corner, they recognized a familiar landmark: the area where they'd spotted Johnny Gunn's stash of booze and money.

"We have to get out of here," Laura wailed. "We stand a better chance against Bell than against a ghost."

They started to run in the direction of the antechamber through which they'd entered, but Will slowed his pace when he felt a breeze nearby. Another escape route? He stopped in his tracks and circled back: It was coming from under the floorboards. With Laura beside him, Will knelt down on the ground and brushed away the dirt to discover another trap door.

He heaved it open to find a ladder descending into a hole. "It's a tunnel. Maybe we can get outside through it." He looked over at Laura, awaiting her decision.

"Some choice!" she said, a **sardonic** edge to her voice. "Crazy men trying to kill us versus evil spirit trying to kill us versus whatever's behind door number three." She moved to the ladder and climbed onto it. "Whatever. This can't possibly get any worse."

She plunged into the darkness, and Will followed after her, hoping she hadn't spoken prematurely.

CHAPTER TWENTY-FOUR

Reaching the bottom rung of the ladder, Will and Laura stepped onto moist ground. It was cold, and already covered with goosebumps from fear, they could do nothing to shake the chill.

No more than six feet wide, the passageway was moldy and **porous**. A cobweb-infested pushcart lay on its side near the ladder, and workmen's lamps were **deployed** at intervals of 100 feet. It appeared to stretch on for miles, no end in sight.

They decided to follow the passageway south, away from the manor. "Who do you think made this tunnel?" Laura asked as they navigated around a puddle of water.

"I'm not sure," Will answered, his voice echoing through the **subterranean** corridor. Noting the dusty liquor bottles that were strewn on either side of their path, he **surmised**, "If it wasn't McAllister, then it was Gunn. One thing's for sure, though.

Whoever did make it didn't tell anyone. If McAllister's servants had known about it, then it'd be common knowledge today."

"I'm thinking McAllister built it so he could sneak around the estate. I mean, we know he was a creep, right? He had an affair with Anna but covered it up. Having this tunnel was probably some sort of power trip. He could show up anywhere on his property without warning."

Laura's **conjecture** sounded **plausible** to Will. The more he'd learned about the founder of Red Fork, the more he believed the worst about him. This tunnel was just the latest evidence of McAllister's **depravity**.

This was no ordinary tunnel they had run into. It seemed a complex network of interconnected **conduits** that stretched out beneath town. At a **confluence** where several other similar channels merged, someone had tacked barely **legible** signs describing where each one led: "Boathouse," "Coal Storage," "Gatehouse," "Guesthouse."

The handwritten signs appeared to be a later addition to the tubes. Will looked at a pile of broken bottles and near them a set of tracks that had been worn into the wood planking. Remembering the pushcart they'd seen near the ladder, he **inferred** that Johnny Gunn had also discovered these tunnels and used them to move his merchandise. So this was the secret to Gunn's **vaunted** ability to operate his illegal business without alerting the police. He didn't have to bribe them with cases of liquor. He trafficked his alcohol right under their noses—literally—moving the cargo from Stone Manor to the coal bins in Sal's Pizzeria and then to the boathouse for shipment up the river. All through these tunnels.

"Which way should we go?" Laura asked. In the bitter underground air, Will could see her breath as she spoke.

"Let's take this one," he said, pointing to one tunnel.

"Are you sure that's a good idea? That's Town Hall." She paused for effect. "You know—where the police station is."

Will shrugged, "It's the last place they'd look for us."

Laura smirked, "That's some pretty lame reasoning. Seriously, was that an **arbitrary** decision or is there something at Town Hall you wanted to—"

Before she could finish her remark, a gust of wind blew out of the main channel, followed by a thunderous roar. The spirit had found them. "Never mind. I hope you're right about the police station."

Me too, he thought as they scurried into the dimly lit corridor. They ran **indefatigably** for almost a mile, driven by fear and adrenaline, and followed the tunnel as it snaked through numerous curves. They passed through sections where all the bulbs had burned out, blindly pushing on and away from the source of the rumble. When they could no longer hear the threatening sound, they slowed, gasping for air.

They trudged on and came to a steep drop. So deep, they couldn't see the bottom of the landing. Complicating the matter further, the wood planks lining their path were slick with moisture, and in the face of treacherous footing, they clung to the crevices in the wall.

As Will stepped cautiously down the boards, a shiver went up his spine. Something or someone was in there with them. Laura glanced over her shoulder, sensing an invisible **predator** lurking behind, and the sudden movement set her off-balance. Her body jerked forward and she screamed as she lost her footing and tumbled down the tunnel. Will moved to catch her, but a blast of wind propelled him forward. In desperation, he reached up to find a recess in the wall and regain his foothold, but there was none. His torso twisted as he too **plummeted** headlong into the dark abyss.

As he plunged down the slope, Will instinctively buried his chin into his chest and flung his arms over his head and neck. A semester's worth of judo in junior high had **inculcated** in him the proper way to take a fall, and he narrowly avoided breaking his neck. He crashed to a halt.

"Are you okay?" Will crawled to Laura and lifted her head to see a trickle of blood seeping from her nose.

"Yeah," she said, wiping the blood with her finger. "I don't think anything's broken … just very bent." She rubbed her neck and then groaned as Will helped her to her feet. "I take it all back. It's definitely worse down here," she said, **retracting** the sarcastic remark she'd made before they entered the tunnels.

They were anxious to get out of there, and with a little rebalancing, resumed their escape. They could hear water dripping into an unseen puddle. At first only a trickle, its **cadence** grew until a steady stream was pouring into the chamber. They ran to the other end of the corridor where another doorway marked the entrance to the next section of the tunnel. Locked.

Now they were wading through several inches of water, a small pool becoming a gushing river in a matter of seconds. The **frenzied** torrent knocked Will and Laura off their feet, tossing them back and forth. Water started jetting in from the holes in the walls at full force, and the room quickly became **deluged**.

Treading water was the only choice now. They swam to the door that they'd previously found locked and tried to shove it open, but it was locked from the other side. Laura dove under the water to search for another means of escape. The tide kept rising, and by the time she resurfaced, only a few inches of air remained at the top of the tunnel. "There's a small tube near the door," she gasped. "I think I can fit through it." When Will didn't respond, Laura understood his **quagmire**: he wouldn't be able to follow her because he was still a mere **neophyte** at swimming and couldn't hold his breath for long. Offering a solution, Laura offered to swim to the other side and open the door. Without hesitation, she inhaled a deep breath and submerged.

Will was **enervated**. He struggled to stay afloat, angling his head upward to keep his nose and mouth at the **acme** of his body. There was no sign of Laura, and she had been under for more than a minute. Will filled his lungs with air one last time and let himself **founder** beneath the surface. It seemed **inevitable** that he would drown, so he took the risk.

The tide suddenly shifted, and Will found himself being pulled through to the next section of the tunnel. The water quickly drained off, depositing him on the floor and leaving scattered puddles as the only **diluvial** evidence. Will panted loudly, gulping in mouthfuls of air until he was no longer wheezing.

"You did it!" he shouted. Wanting to shower her with **accolades** for her **mettle**, he scanned his new surroundings. "Laura?" There was no reply. He was alone in the tunnel.

CHAPTER TWENTY-FIVE

Maybe she went on ahead. After calling out to Laura a dozen times, Will gave up, his anxious cries met only by indifferent silence. With a **kernel** of hope, he raced through the passageway, his wet sneakers squishing on the floorboards. He ached to rest, but the **noisome** smell of decay forced him on.

He thought about the series of events that had led him to this point, and regretted having gone down there at all. *We should have taken our chances with Bell and Tompkins. At least then Laura and I wouldn't have gotten separated and she'd still be with me.* The what-ifs ran through his mind, and he felt totally to blame. *I should've just let it alone. I'd be blissfully ignorant and I'd have fit in all these years.*

Anger and self-**loathing** welled up inside. He **abhorred** everything about Will Lassiter—the "freak" who mowed Monets into lawns; the **retiring** boy so disconnected; the descendant of a killer. It was murder, no matter how **vindictive** McAllister was or how much he deserved it. How could Will **atone** for the sins of his great-grandfather? He heard a voice call his name, and thought it was McAllister again. Inflamed, he yelled into the darkness, "Leave me alone!"

Then he heard the voice again. "Will!" This wasn't the phantom. It was an urgent cry from Laura. She was alive!

"I'm here," he called back, a huge sense of relief warming his chilled body. "Where are you?"

"I'm in a tunnel," Laura said without a trace of **irony**. "I'm so glad to hear your voice. I was afraid you didn't make it."

In order to trace her voice, Will urged Laura to keep talking. "Okay, so what's it like in your tunnel? Mine is heated, smells like fresh flowers, and there's a big refrigerator full of food. Mmm!" Will followed the sound of her voice to a nearby wall. She was on the other side in another passage.

Now they had to figure out how to meet up. At first, Will tried digging at the wall, but seeing that an impossible task, they decided to move forward. Maybe they'd merge up ahead. They spent the time calling out to each other, though not without a dose of fun.

"Marco!"

"Polo," she responded in kind. He could hear her distinctive laugh through the thick wall of earth. She began to sing the chorus to "Hey Jude," and he joined in. They kept their course, with the

Beatles' melody reverberating through both tunnels. Noticing that their voices were growing more faint, Laura concluded, "My tunnel is turning around. I think it's going back toward the manor. What should we do?"

By now, Will could barely hear her, but he understood enough to respond. "Just keep going," he shouted at the top of his lungs. "Get to my house and find my parents. Tell them what's going on. And wait for me. I'll find my way out and sneak back there. Then we'll all go to the state police."

Will couldn't hear Laura's reply. He could only hope she had heard him. **Rejuvenated** by the fact that Laura was safe, he doubled his pace: He'd find an exit to the surface, rejoin Laura, and they'd report Bell and Tompkins to the proper authorities.

Will gathered that he was now under Town Hall, the narrow passage widening into a circular space. A ladder caught his eye, though upon climbing it, the hatch held fast. Muddled voices on the other side suggested a town meeting in progress. *Probably everyone in Red Fork is there. Including Mom and Dad!*

He banged on the trap door, his **clamoring** unheard. It dawned on him that he was probably below the basement of the building where the jail was. Since most residents of Red Fork were law-abiding citizens, likely no one was down there to hear him. As he was steeling himself to push open the door, Will felt another breeze. *McAllister again?* His heart skipped a beat in fear, but then his nose picked up a sharp odor. Gas! The room was filling up with the poisonous fumes. Looking up to the pipes, Will's eyes zeroed in on one valve: It was turning by itself and releasing the gas into the chamber.

The spigot was just beyond Will's reach, and the threat of asphyxia catapulted him into throwing all his weight against the trap door. He became lightheaded but pressed on, determined to push his way through or pass out trying. It was an **onerous** task, but the trap door—not to mention the linoleum tiles from above—eventually gave way. He had finally broken through to the basement of Town Hall.

He drank in the **toxin**-free air as he crawled from the hole, but before he could rest, he heard a familiar hiss. A mass of electric wiring was snaking out of the relay box on the wall, as if some invisible force was pulling at it. Gas began to **infiltrate** the room, which terrified Will, as he knew any sort of spark would ignite it.

It could only be McAllister. He was trying to **obliterate** Town Hall, just as he did to the boathouse and Sal's. But this time, human life was at risk—that of all the townsfolk, including Ken and Joanne. Will knew what was at stake, and he had to act fast.

He rushed toward the box, trying to shut off the power. But as he got within arm's length, the loosened wires ensnared him. The thick cords quickly **incapacitated** him, and his swift and **canny** move to wedge his hands between the wires and his neck was all that prevented him from being choked. He watched in horror as the wires leading into the bottom of the relay box became taut: McAllister was about to sever their connection from the box. Will squirmed, freeing his lower body, and just as the phantom yanked out the wires, he swung his leg up and kicked the kill-switch to "Off."

The room went dark. The electrical circuit to the entire building had been cut. Will felt something brush by him, the cold presence he was certain was McAllister. A gust of wind followed, sucking the contaminated air into the tunnels and slamming the trap door shut as the spirit fled back to Stone Manor.

Will next heard a low moan followed by the rattle of a steel chain. It was growing louder and more insistent, and Will wished he could melt into the wall. Suddenly, the **auxiliary** lights kicked in, illuminating the space just well enough for Will to make out the silhouette of a figure hunched over in a corner.

The shape **writhed** as it moaned incomprehensibly. It was a desperate wail. Slowly the sound became more recognizable as a word, and then more specifically a name: "Will!"

It was Dr. Perez! Bound and gagged, he stared pleadingly at Will. Moving quickly to remove the duct tape from his mouth, Will **emancipated** him from his incarceration, helping a **debilitated** Perez to his feet. The first thing he asked for was Laura.

With his parents probably upstairs, Will explained she was fine. He quickly changed the topic. "Who did this to you?"

None other than Daniel Bell. "Bell?" Then, remembering the **curator's erratic** behavior, he understood. "Of course! He was chasing us all over the place too, and with the sheriff's help! We had just come back from the orphanage—"

"The orphanage? How did you—?" Perez looked startled momentarily and then **enjoined** with a sudden burst of energy, "What did you find out?"

Will filled him in on the details: how they had found Perez's journal in order to look for him, how they found out about the orphanage, and how they had learned Anna Krause left a baby named Elizabeth.

But who was the father, Perez wanted to know?

"The record didn't say. But we think it was McAllister." Will tried to redirect the conversation back to their immediate situation. "Do you have any idea what's made Mr. Bell go crazy all of a sudden?"

"I'm not sure, but I have a theory," Perez said as he moved toward the door. "Help me get this open. We have to get upstairs as soon as possible."

CHAPTER TWENTY-SIX

Will entered the meeting hall a step behind Dr. Perez. The emergency lighting had kicked in up here as well, and people were rushing to get out of the building. Sheer **anarchy**.

The crowd turned and gaped at Will and Dr. Perez. Since the historian's disappearance had made him a celebrity in town, he was quickly mobbed. People slapped him on the back, **lionizing** him as if he were a returning war hero.

Will's parents spotted him, too, and they rapidly approached.

"Where have you been?" Joanne asked angrily.

Ken joined his mother in **berating** him. "William, you're in big trouble! You can't just drive off like that—you don't even have a license!"

Before Will could answer, the crowd shushed as Dr. Perez prepared to speak. He was up on the stage now, standing near the mayor. The townsfolk faced him, eager to know what had happened. In an even tone, he began, "I was kidnapped by Daniel Bell and Sheriff Tompkins."

A ripple of reactions spread around the room. Shocked, no doubt, some people **scoffed**, others cried out. Most, however, remained silent, waiting for the rest of the story.

Dr. Perez continued. "They, along with Harold Dittlemeyer and Sal Mannino, belong to an organization called The Ring of McAllister. It is some sort of **covert** group, though I'm not entirely certain what it is that they're hiding, other than the fact that Algernon McAllister is not the saint you all know and **revere** him as. I've been researching the man and have discovered some alarming facts about him—**discrepancies** that suggest he's the **antithesis** of the Historical Society's rosy portrait. It appears I got too close to the truth, and Bell panicked. So he and the sheriff grabbed me off the street the other day and imprisoned me downstairs in a room next to the jail."

So that's what The Ring was, thought Will. *It makes sense, in light of how the* **coterie** *tried to intimidate me after I found out about Anna Krause and her baby.*

"I was shackled down there all this time, and I shudder to think of what they ultimately would have done, were it not for my rescue by a very bright and resourceful young man—" Perez nodded at his liberator, "Will Lassiter."

A smattering of applause could be heard as Will joined Dr. Perez onstage. He cleared his throat and leaned into the microphone. "He's telling the truth. I found him tied up in the basement." He addressed his parents directly, knowing they would believe him, and added, "Bell threatened me and Laura too. He and the sheriff chased us all over town."

"How dare you accuse me!" Bell cried. He had taken notice of all the stares. "That man is a **fraud**. He probably staged this whole disappearance as a publicity stunt. He said it himself: He's writing a book about McAllister. All this **notoriety** will help put him on the best-seller list, no doubt. He has **duped** us. For all we know, he blew up the boathouse himself. It all fits the profile of this **charlatan**."

As soon as Bell's **diatribe** ended, Will quickly spoke up. "No, that was McAllister! His spirit, I mean. He's the one responsible for all the explosions. I saw it myself just now down in the secret tunnels. He was turning on the gas line and then he tried to start a spark from some electrical wiring. I had to turn off the main power, which is why we're sitting here in the dark. McAllister did the same thing with the boathouse and Sal's. He was able to get to all those places by these tunnels that run underground across the whole town."

"Ghosts? Secret tunnels?" Bell **belittled** Will's **assertion**. "You'll have to do better than that, Mr. Lassiter. For what Perez is probably paying you to back up his wild claims, your story should be more **credible**. That said, I do appreciate your creative imagination. It provides us all with some much-needed amusement!" He smirked at Will and then looked out over the audience for support.

Unfortunately, the crowd was **inclined** to believe Bell. After all, he was one of their own, and nothing in his past suggested that he was anything but an expert on the subject of Algernon McAllister. Will knew that in the end, this was what he and Perez were up against—a century's worth of lies that had **obfuscated** the true nature of the "**Paragon** of Red Fork." Any unkind words about the man would be viewed as **blasphemous**. The only way to combat Bell was to challenge his **verity** and then **discredit** him.

"What about Anna Krause?" Will asked in an even-mannered tone.

Bell hesitated for a moment before throwing the question right back at him. "What about her?" He stared meaningfully at Will, who in turn caught Bell's meaning. If they were going to bring up the subject of Anna, then the subject of Henry Lassiter's brutal act would also come out.

If Bell thought this **defamatory insinuation** would silence Will, he was wrong. "I'm not afraid of the truth," he said, returning the steely gaze. "Why, are you?"

While Bell revealed no outward discomfort, his hesitation in answering spoke to his **complicity**. The crowd murmured in surprise. Finally, the sheriff stood up. "Dan, I think it's time we came clean. This has gone too far." He looked down at the floor.

In the eyes of the audience, the sheriff's plea amounted to a confession, and the people standing near him backed away, distancing themselves from the **contrite** but guilty lawman. Noticing the effect of his words, his face took on a pained expression, and he looked sorrowfully at his wife. "We kidnapped Perez. Just like he said. And, yes, we're part of The Ring. We're a small group dedicated to protecting the legacy of Algernon McAllister." He took off his hat and rubbed the back of his neck. "We didn't mean any harm. We're good citizens. This just got out of hand." He turned to Dr. Perez and said, "I'm so very sorry, sir. I hope we didn't…." The words escaped him, and Tompkins could only shake his head in regret. Turning, he surrendered his badge and gun to the mayor and slumped in a folding chair.

Will marveled at the **irony**. All his life he had been the outsider, the **iconoclast** of Red Fork who couldn't wait to escape, but now, he knew more about the town and its history than anyone. In the end, he would be the one to enlighten them about the man they'd **canonized**. "This is what The Ring was trying to hide: McAllister had a maid named Anna Krause, and he got her pregnant. But after the baby was born, McAllister tried to kill it." As he spoke, Will replayed the infant's wailing from his dreams, and he was momentarily stuck trying to comprehend such an act. But then, envisioning the scene, he could hear McAllister's reaction. "He was ashamed of the child because it wasn't 'a pure-bred aristocrat.' It was a 'mongrel' and didn't deserve to live." Will spoke in a dull monotone because the only way to get out McAllister's hate-filled descriptions was by first numbing himself. He glanced over at Bell, waiting for the local historian to deny the statement. But Bell, his lips pursed, conveyed only a strange **ambivalence** to the account.

"But Anna fought back," Will continued, "And McAllister strangled her to death." He looked at his neighbors before glancing at his father. He knew the next part would be hardest for him to hear. "My great-grandfather, Henry Lassiter, was also there. He tried to stop McAllister. They fought, and McAllister was killed. If you don't believe me, there are two bodies buried in back of Stone Manor—Anna and McAllister. We found their skeletons." Will turned back to **castigate** Bell. "If this is what you were protecting, why?"

The mayor also wanted to know, and as if his inquiry lent the scene more authority, the crowd shifted its gaze. They all looked at Bell, ready for him to **capitulate**.

Bell was almost **repentant**. "Okay … yes … it's all just as Will said. After McAllister died, Henry wanted to turn himself in for the murder." Bell glared at Will and Ken, and added accusingly, "I think the Lassiters have always been weak. Had Henry gone to the authorities and told them it was an accident—which it was—what chance would he have had that they'd believe him, a lowly butler? That's what the other servants argued too, and they convinced Henry rightfully that the best thing to do was cover up the murders. So they buried the bodies and sent the child to an orphanage. They then told anyone who asked that McAllister had gone to Europe for the season. When the Titanic sank a few months later, they had the perfect situation for his death. There would be no body, and thus no **inquest**. My great-grandfather, Clayton Bell, was able to alter documents to make it appear McAllister was on the ship. He even perfected McAllister's signature."

"What about the will?" The mayor asked. "Didn't McAllister leave Red Fork to his servants?"

Bell laughed: It turns out, McAllister had no will. He thought he was going to live forever. "My great-grandfather was the one to **draft** the will. He gave the estate to our ancestors. He knew that the servants were all simple people, without prospects in the world. What would become of them if they had to leave Red Fork? Clayton Bell created this town." The audience was engrossed. "You didn't know that, did you? Of course not. Want to know why?" He was on a roll now, **ranting** at the crowd. "Your grandparents and great-grandparents agreed to keep this from everyone, including their own children. A select few were chosen to protect the truth and create an alternative story, one of a thoughtful McAllister **bequeathing** his vast estate to his loyal servants. From generation to generation, The Ring of McAllister has been **vigilant**, maintaining the honor and order in the town, always knowing that if the truth came out it would destroy us. And now, despite all my efforts, it did."

Bell bore down on Will, "Now do you see what you've done? You and your family have **blighted** this town. You've shamed us all."

Will scanned the faces of his neighbors but could detect no bitterness. They were bewildered, as if they'd just awoken from a troubled sleep. "No," Will turned back to Bell. "It was your ancestor who shamed us. My great-grandfather stood up for the truth. The truth isn't going to destroy this town. It's going to set us free."

He looked back over the audience amassed along the **convex** edge of the stage. Their apprehensive expressions reminded him of the faces in his final dream, and he suddenly felt the same electric connection to the community he had experienced then. He began to understand why the townspeople of today were in that nightmare about the past. They represented their ancestors, the "simple servants" who had acted in **collusion** to cover up Henry Lassiter's sin. By conspiring to hide the murders, these good people had become **unwitting** accomplices and then fell prone to **inevitable** guilt. By escaping the law—and blame—they bowed to the pressure on their consciences. *It's not that no one ever wants to leave Red Fork,* it dawned on Will. *It's ingrained in them that they should stay.* Without hope or knowledge of **absolving** themselves from the sins of their forefathers, they were bound to this small speck of Pennsylvania land.

Will wanted to convey this notion to the **aggregate** of Red Fork residents, but he had to choose his words carefully. "I wonder, does it strike any of you as bizarre that in the hundred years or so that this town has existed, none of our ancestors has ever moved away? Wouldn't you think at least one person would want to see what's out there beyond McAllister Boulevard?" The servants' guilt had become a something of a genetic **malediction**, passed down in each generation, believed Will.

While most of the audience stared at him blankly, overwhelmed, a few nodded, acknowledging Will's words. He felt relieved and **vindicated** by their reaction. At least some would accept the truth, and perhaps slowly, the belief would **disseminate** across town. But whatever the outcome, he was at peace. Finally, he wasn't an outcast for having a desire to see the world—it was a perfectly normal aspiration. *But why was I immune to it?* As if in response to his question, Will felt a surge of pain in his arm, and when he glanced down, he had his answer. When he'd been scarred by McAllister's spirit, he saw the truth in a flurry of disturbing images and was freed from the unconscious **penance** as a result. They'd revisited him in his nightmares, growing clearer each time as they slowly revealed what had really happened in Stone Manor all those years ago. And now everyone else knew. Things would never be the same. He faced Bell and the crowd and **avowed**, "We're all free. Finally free."

CHAPTER TWENTY-SEVEN

Despite Will's declaration, Daniel Bell may have proved **prescient** about Red Fork's demise. Most of the people in the hall remained frozen in their places. Will had **attested** to the true history of the town, and he hoped his neighbors would accept his revelation and move on from it. His small group of supporters **rallied** around him. Nearly as many others began to cry. Still others **rued** allowing an **interloper** like Dr. Perez to tear down the community with his **chicanery**.

After a long period of consideration, the mayor decided to **arbitrate**. "Okay folks, settle down. What I'd like to know is, how did you figure all this out? Because if it's true, there's been some fine detective work here." His **liberal** tone suggested that he was, at the very least, willing to entertain their notion.

Will wasn't prepared to admit that his involvement in the investigation grew out of his nightmares. That sort of **psychic** mumbo-jumbo wouldn't likely be embraced by many of the town's residents, so he **relegated** the task of explaining to Dr. Perez.

"After my wife died, I realized how little I knew about her roots. Her parents had both died before we met, and Ellie never spoke much about her family. I wanted Laura to know her own heritage, so I took it upon myself to research my wife's history. I traced her family back to Chicago where her grandmother had grown up. Her grandmother had been adopted. I made inquiries, but the birth records from that long ago were scarce and so I thought I'd reached the end of the line. But then I found the ring."

He put his hand in his shirt pocket and pulled out a jewel-encrusted ring. The workmanship was exquisite. "This had been passed down from my wife's grandmother to her mother and then on to my wife. It now belongs to Laura. It was the only family heirloom Ellie had." He rubbed the band between his fingers. "It was so **ostentatious**, gaudy really, and Ellie's family was far from wealthy, so we assumed it was just a piece of costume jewelry."

"But while in Chicago, I came across an exhibit about Algernon McAllister. There was a description of his fabled ring, and it matched this one perfectly." He closed his fist around the ring. "So I had our ring appraised and learned that it was worth a not-so-small fortune! All the gems were indeed genuine. It struck me as an odd coincidence and an even more fantastic connection—what did one of the richest men in America have in common with an orphan in Chicago? I went into full research mode on McAllister, even moving here to where he lived, so I could find the link between him and my wife's grandmother." He held his fist up. "This was all I had to go on."

After Dr. Perez traced how his **matrilineal** line of inquiry had taken him and Laura from Arizona to Chicago and then to Red Fork, he revealed that, in this tiny enclave, he had finally found his answer. "Ellie's grandmother was Elizabeth, the child of Anna Krause and Algernon McAllister. She was left at the orphanage with this ring as the only symbol **betokening** her to her natural parents." He nodded at Will, acknowledging him for this, the final piece to the puzzle.

For Will, Perez's pronouncement had the reciprocal effect of providing him much-needed **clarity**. He thought he had mistaken Anna for Laura in his dreams, but he now understood that the two women were **cognate**. Laura's arrival in Red Fork hadn't coincided with the start of his nightmares; it had been the **catalyst** for them. Her relation to Anna had awakened his **primordial** visions, which then **manifested** themselves in the form of nightmares.

"What about the explosions at Sal's and the boathouse?" Dolores's gruff voice boomed through the room. "We never got clear-cut answers about what happened. All I know is these troubles started after the Perezes moved here, and I see nothing to change that view." Dolores had made her agenda clear. In order to maintain the status quo, she would attack anyone who challenged it.

Will considered Dolores's claim, then summarily dismissed it. "As I've already said, that was the ghost!" he **rebutted** back.

"Ghosts again?" Bell **mocked**, glad to have an opportunity to retaliate and **vilify** Will's **credibility**.

Ignoring him, Will continued. "Dolores has a point, sort of. Those incidents didn't happen until after the Perezes moved here. It's not a coincidence. But they didn't **instigate** the explosions. I think their presence in the manor, or really Laura's presence, somehow woke up McAllister's ghost." As he spoke, Will was **formulating** in his mind how this really could be the case. The spirit had lain there, weak, for years, terrorizing only those in direct contact. That's what happened to him as a young boy. But the **consanguineous** bond between Laura and McAllister had renewed the phantom's strength, and with this new power, it was able to rove the town and lash out at the people of Red Fork.

Will tried to position his argument into words people would understand. "We all know the story about the two kids who went into Stone Manor and disappeared, right?" Will scanned the room until he found his oldest friend. "I was lucky enough to get away. McAllister wants revenge on all of us." Will held up his scar for all to see.

Dolores remained unconvinced: She wanted to know why McAllister hadn't just come to her house and killed her.

"I don't know," Ty replied, jumping up onto the stage. "Maybe he will," he quipped, squeezing Will's shoulder.

Will took Dolores' statement more seriously. As a child, he recalled feeling safe once he was out of the mansion. And somehow, he had known that McAllister couldn't follow him out.

He addressed Dolores. "I don't think he can get to you. His spirit is trapped in the manor."

"Then how did he get to the boathouse and Sal's?"

The answer was obvious to Will. He had just been down there. "The tunnels. They connect the mansion to various parts of the original estate." McAllister had moved through them like a virus that courses through the veins of a body, attacking the town in a **pique** of vengeance.

Bell's supporters hoped he'd **discredit** Will's theory, but he could offer nothing concrete. "There have long been rumors of secret passages under the town. I can neither confirm nor deny their existence." His words served to strengthen Will's argument.

"I've seen the spirit too," Dr. Perez said. "Or rather, I've seen what it can do. It's been trying to harm Laura. At first I thought my presence could protect her, but after what happened at the boathouse, I sent her away from Stone Manor." He looked into the crowd. "Laura? Where are you, dear?"

Will looked to his parents, expecting their input.

"We haven't seen her since last night," Ken said.

Dr. Perez turned on Bell. "What have you done with her? If you've harmed her in any way...."

Bell shook his head, claiming he hadn't seen her. Perez didn't believe him. He rushed at Bell and grabbed him by the neck. "What have you done with my daughter, you son of.... Tell me! Tell me!"

His face flushed and his voice stifled by the choking, Bell whispered, "N-nothing. I swear, I have no idea … no idea where she is."

Tompkins pulled Perez off Bell and said to the enraged historian, "Sir, we didn't take your daughter. You have my word on that. Please, calm down." Although he was no longer the sheriff, he still retained his authoritative manner. When Perez had softened his grip on Bell, Tompkins faced the crowd. "Has anyone seen Laura Perez?"

There was no response from the audience, so Will stepped forward to disclose more. "We got separated in the tunnels. I told her to go back to my house…." His voice trailed off as he pictured Laura alone in the underground corridors. In his mind, Will saw her walking through a darkened hallway. Then he envisioned a dark figure coming up behind her. Shuddering, he knew exactly where she was. "Omigosh, she never got out! Laura is in Stone Manor. And she's in trouble!"

There was no debate this time—no question of Will's **veracity**, no lingering doubt due to his being a "freak." He and Dr. Perez climbed into a police car with Tompkins and sped off to the mansion.

Will leapt from the vehicle before it came to a stop, Dr. Perez just two steps behind. They raced to the door. Will slipped in first, though the others were too late. The door slammed closed. The shutters banged closed. Will would have to save Laura by himself.

CHAPTER TWENTY-EIGHT

Pounding on the door, Perez and Tompkins tried desperately to get into the manor. The door and the windows were locked. So, too, were they from the inside. Everything was bolted shut. Will knew he'd have to **infiltrate** McAllister's keep on his own, and there was no time to waste.

Stepping into the **capacious** center room, Will was uncertain of how to proceed. He closed his eyes, thinking he'd heighten his other senses. Drowning out the noises from outside, he listened for clues. He first went to the right, thinking he'd heard something there. But as he went toward the dining room, that door slammed shut. He backed off and headed toward the den. That door, too, closed quickly. And then, he heard a decided creak ahead of him, the tinny sound of a rusted hinge.

It came from behind the stairwell, Will was sure, the door that went to the basement. He peered into the darkness, "Laura?"

There was no reply. The basement door inched open a little more. He called out again for Laura, and again, was answered with silence. *Someone's trying to tell me something.* Mistrustful of whatever it was, Will felt around in the dark until his hands closed around a broom handle. Gripping it tightly, he stepped over the threshold. He found the light switch, turned it on, and descended the stairs.

As soon as he reached the bottom, the door locked behind him. There was no choice now but to go forward. In fact, a path had been cleared for him. He walked cautiously across the basement, toward the **niche** where he and Laura had hidden from Bell. When he got to the compartment, he crouched down and looked inside. The wooden planks had been torn **asunder** and left in a heap, leaving him to see right into the secret hallway that led to the servants' quarters and library. He crawled through.

Although only a few hours had elapsed since he and Laura first traveled in this corridor, it seemed much longer to Will. The place seemed only vaguely familiar, the passage narrower and walls darker than he remembered. The air felt heavy. He stepped over the trap door to the tunnels and then past closed doors on either side of him. They were all locked. He rounded a corner and saw a flicker of light from underneath the last door on the right. It was the library, the room where McAllister had killed Anna and then died at the hands of Henry Lassiter. Will turned the doorknob, expecting it to be locked as well. In fact, it opened easily. And there, in the corner weeping, was Laura. Will rushed to her quickly.

"Will?" When she lifted her head, he saw numerous scratches and bruises on her **wan** face and neck. "Thank goodness!" she hugged him tightly. "How did you get in?"

Will shook off the question, in haste to get them out. He helped her to her feet, but then, a blast of cold air stopped them. The door slammed shut, and the wind continued to whirl all around them. *McAllister.* The gust picked up speed and strength, tossing books and chairs all over the room. It became a **juggernaut.** Holding Laura with one arm, Will clutched the mantle for support with the other, though to no **avail.** He lost his grip, and the fierce tornado **buffeted** them about the library. After what felt like several minutes, the thrashing **subsided.**

But the **insidious** ghost was with them, inside of the room. The dark figure lunged forward, sending Will flying across the floor. Before he could recover, the silhouette disappeared into the shadows, only to reappear a moment later. This time, though, it took on **corporeal** form.

This was the man who stalked him in his sleep, Will knew: It was McAllister **incarnate.** He wore the same sneer curved across his lips as in Will's dream and stood looming over them in his spotless dark topcoat, a red ascot looped around his neck. He ignored Will's coiled stance and **assailed** Laura in his chilling baritone, "Where is she?" Laura shrank back, intimidated by the robber-baron's **imposing** demeanor. In a rage, McAllister scooped her up off the floor and shook her, "Where is the child?"

Will had seen all this before—in his dreams. This was a replay of the struggle 90 years earlier. Laura represented Anna, and he was Henry. Violent images from his haunting dreams flashed before his eyes and then **coalesced** into a single reality: Here and now, he had to stop McAllister.

"Leave her alone!" he thundered, grabbing the broom. It served him for two blows to McAllister's midsection, but then was promptly snatched away and tossed into the fire.

With no other weapon at his disposal, Will resorted to brute force. He lunged at McAllister's feet, knocking him off-balance. The robber-baron righted himself just as Will barreled into him again, this time using his shoulder to ram into McAllister's side. But Will's **vulnerable** position proved **advantageous** to his foe. He gripped Will in a headlock and then flung him against a wall.

As a dazed Will struggled to remain conscious from his concussion, McAllister turned back to Laura. His dark eyes glowing, he stretched his arms out in a direct line for her neck. Laura begged for her life. "No ... please no ...," she pleaded, backing away from the **burly** man. McAllister was within fingers' reach of her **larynx** when an unsteady Will tackled him from behind. Staggering against the teenager's weight, McAllister twisted around, grabbed him by the waist, and started pushing him toward the fire. The flames grew nearer as Will struggled in vain. Feeling the intense heat against his back, he was **spurred** by fear to turn his body around, reversing positions with McAllister just as his great-grandfather had done. The thrust of Will's defensive movement sent his adversary careening toward the fireplace, but this time, McAllister anticipated the reaction and knew how to combat it. He threw his arms up to prevent his head from colliding with the mantle and recovered. Spinning around, his **incarnadine** face was stoked by rage, and he hissed furiously, "Lassiter!"

Meanwhile, Laura had run to the door and yanked it open. "Will!" she shouted, motioning for him to join her. He scurried across the room, and they escaped into the hallway with an **incensed** McAllister in close pursuit.

Will led Laura through the corridor as the walls rumbled around them. McAllister's maniacal laugh echoed in their ears. They ran fast, past swinging doors and through a **cacophony** of noise. Suddenly, just when they had found an exit, McAllister was bearing down on them.

The cruelty on his face froze Will and Laura into submission. They slid down into a sitting position and clasped their arms around one other. Every bone in Will's body screamed out in pain; he just didn't have the energy to fight anymore. Despite everything they'd done, McAllister would get his revenge after all: He'd kill the descendant of his killer and the only evidence of his **impropriety** in one fell swoop.

Will's scar throbbed, more intensely than it ever had before. **Mocking** him one last time, it reminded him of his many shortcomings and ultimate inability to fend off this **inevitable** fate. He waited for McAllister's deathblow.

But just before the robber-baron reached them, a woman's voice **rebuked** him. It was the same voice Laura had heard weeks earlier, when McAllister had tried to choke her. For Will, too, this was the sweet tone guiding him to safety all those years ago.

"Mom?"

McAllister whirled around, only to find a slender woman glaring at him. The two teens gazed on their savior, and indeed the similarities between Laura's mother and this woman were striking. Anna Krause herself had come to their rescue. It wasn't Laura's mother after all. It was her great-grandmother.

Anna's eyes met those of her **progeny**, and her loving gaze filled Laura's heart. There was nothing Laura could do except stare back at her ancestor's **benign** form. Anna smiled, understanding Laura's surprise, and then **diverted** her eyes. Turning to McAllister, she commanded, "You will not harm her." Before the robber-baron had a chance to object, Anna plowed into him, shoving him away. Will and Laura were able to flee.

McAllister and Anna struggled, leaving Will no choice but to help. **Obdurate**, he couldn't let McAllister kill her. But before he could make a move to save her, Anna locked eyes with him, and in that instant, he understood: She was sacrificing herself for the liberation of her child. For as long as McAllister was wrestling with her, he couldn't hurt Laura. Anna wanted Will to scoop Laura away to safety and far from Stone Manor.

Summoning the last of her energy, Anna clasped her hands around McAllister's neck while keeping her eyes squarely on Will. He nodded at her and swiftly led Laura out of the corridor, never once looking back.

Retracing the escape route he'd taken seven years before, Will led Laura toward safety, and again, with Anna's help. *Hurry Will, hurry.* The townsfolk could be heard banging on the front door.

For a moment, they were **thwarted**. The front door wouldn't budge and a bloodcurdling howl shook the house. A gust of wind passed through the room. *Anna must have lost her battle,* **surmised** Will. But unexpectedly, the door to the basement slammed shut, and the front door opened. Will and Laura rushed through the entranceway and into the arms of their relieved parents.

"I know, Dad. I thought I lost you, too." Laura collapsed in his arms. And then, looking into her father's eyes, "I'm glad we came to Red Fork. I'm glad I finally met Mom's side of the family."

As Will was being smothered by his mother's kisses, he couldn't stop thinking: What had become of Anna and McAllister? He felt **compelled** to go back in and help her—he owed it to her, after all, and to Henry Lassiter. Untangling himself from his parents' arms, he started back toward the front porch, but before he could reach the first step, the door slammed shut … for the last time.

That night, Will was back in his bedroom, staring out the window at the **adjacent** property. He had just completed what would be his final sketch of the manor. In it, the windows were no longer eyes bearing down on him as they'd been in earlier, more **anthropomorphic** drawings. He'd stripped away the detailing of his previous works, and now presented the manor as a single stone structure without any openings to the world. This was how he would remember it.

No one would ever enter Stone Manor again. Anna's spirit had sealed the house, trapping herself and McAllister in, and keeping innocents out. McAllister's spirit, incapable of being **vanquished**, would remain there, imprisoned forever.

And so too—regrettably—would that of Anna Krause.

EPILOGUE

Summer ended, and Will and his friends returned to school for their senior year. The seasons passed quickly. Spring arrived, and with the **vernal** bloom came college letters in the mail. Katie was accepted into the University of Pittsburgh, and Ty, thanks to his **affinity** with computers, received a full academic scholarship to Stanford—and finally bested his brother at something. In fact, their high school class was the first in the town's history to have any of its graduates **matriculate** to colleges outside of Red Fork.

Laura still wasn't sure what she wanted to major in, so she decided to enroll at McAllister College and remain near her father, who had been appointed an **adjunct** professorship there. As for Will, he followed his passion and pursued a degree in art. **Ironically**, he stayed in Red Fork to attend school with Laura. After they would graduate though, their travels would take them far and wide, with Will living out his global dream.

Daniel Bell and the rest of The Ring were arrested shortly after the final incident at Stone Manor and **indicted** on charges of kidnapping and obstruction of justice. Because the trial took place in Red Fork, Bell was confident of their eventual **acquittal**. But the jury of his **peers** didn't share this view and convicted him and Tompkins on all counts, while the other two **defendants**, Sal Mannino and Harold Dittlemeyer, were shown **clemency** and sentenced only to probation.

The **harrowing** events of that summer brought no immediate **catharsis** in Red Fork. For a while, the townsfolk would only agree to fill in all the underground tunnels—necessary, they claimed, "to **sustain** the structural **integrity**" of the buildings that rested above the **subterranean** corridors. It took many more years for people to come clean and admit that they'd wanted to **consign** McAllister's restless spirit solely to the mansion.

While some hardliners like Dolores stubbornly maintained the **prevarication** of a generous McAllister or *chose* to believe the lie, signs gradually appeared that Will's revelations had indeed **irrevocably** altered the course of the town. Many people **denounced** the robber-baron, and still others put their houses up for sale and moved away.

The blissful ignorance of Red Fork residents was forever gone. No longer satisfied with their simple surroundings, many were **allured** by the more sophisticated trappings of bigger cities. Red

Fork had become too small, too **provincial**, too far removed from both the present and the future.

The truth had set the people free, just as Will had said. But in doing so, the town, like so many of the tiny communities that dot the rural northeast, began to wither away. Over the next several years, more and more people opted to leave, many without even finding a buyer for their homes.

In the end, Red Fork would be left to its ghosts.

APPENDIXES

GLOSSARY

Learning this word list, and command of language in general, includes being able to understand a vocabulary word in its various word forms. So a word that appears here as an adjective, for instance, may be used in the novel in its noun form.

Also, the selected definitions listed here are for words as they're used in the book. For definitions not included here, please consult a dictionary.

A

abandon (*noun*)—total lack of inhibition, unbounded enthusiasm

abase—to humble; disgrace

abate—decrease, reduce

abdicate—to give up a position, right, or power

aberration—a deviation from the proper or expected course

abet—to assist and encourage (as an accomplice)

abhor—to loathe, detest

abject—brought low in condition or status

abortive—failing to accomplish an intended result

abridged—condensed, shortened

abscond—to depart secretly

absolve—to forgive, free from blame

accede—to express approval; agree to

accessible—attainable, available; approachable

accolade—praise, distinction

accost—to approach and speak to someone

accrue—to accumulate, grow by additions

acme—highest point; summit

acquiesce—to accept without opposition; comply quietly

acquittal—release from blame

acrid—harsh, bitter

acrimony—bitterness, animosity

acuity—sharpness of perception or vision

acute—sharp, pointed, severe

adage—old saying or proverb

adamant—uncompromising, unyielding

adapt—to accommodate, adjust

adhere—to hold fast or stick by something, as if by gluing

adjacent—next to

adjunct—added as an auxiliary staff member

admonish—to caution, correct, express disapproval

adroitly—skillfully

adulation—high praise

adumbrate—to sketch or outline in a shadowy way; to foreshadow

advantageous—favorable, useful

aerial—having to do with the air

affable—friendly, easy to approach

affinity—fondness, liking; similarity

affluent—rich, abundant

affront (*noun*)—personal offense, insult

aggregate (*noun*)—collective mass or sum; total

aggrieved—troubled in spirit, distressed

agile—well coordinated, flexible in a graceful way

agitation—commotion, excitement; uneasiness

agrarian—relating to farming or rural matters

ajar—slightly open

algorithm—mechanical problem-solving procedure

alias—an assumed name, false name

alienate—to make unfriendly or hostile where there had formerly been affection

alleviate—to relieve, ease

allude—to make indirect reference; to refer

allure (*verb*)—to entice by charm; attract

aloof—detached, indifferent

altercation—noisy dispute

altruistic—unselfish, concerned for the welfare of others

ambiguous—unclear, subject to multiple interpretations

ambivalence—attitude of uncertainty; conflicting emotions

amend—to improve or correct flaws in

amiable—friendly, pleasant, likable

amicable—friendly, agreeable

amoral—unprincipled, unethical

amorous—strongly attracted to love; showing love

amorphous—having no definite form

ample—abundant, plentiful

amplify—to increase, intensify

anachronism—something chronologically inappropriate

anachronistic—chronologically out of place

analogous—comparable, parallel

anarchy—absence of government or law; chaos

anecdote—short, usually funny account of an event

angular—characterized by sharp angles

animation—enthusiasm, excitement

animosity—hatred, hostility

anodyne—something that calms or soothes pain

anonymity—condition of having no name or an unknown name

antagonist—foe, opponent, adversary

anthropomorphic—attributing human qualities to nonhumans

antipathy—dislike, hostility; extreme opposition or aversion

antiquated—outdated, obsolete

antithesis—exact opposite or direct contrast

apathetic—indifferent, unconcerned

apocryphal—fictitious; of doubtful authenticity

apotheosis—glorification; glorified ideal

appease—to satisfy, placate, calm, pacify

approbation—praise; official approval

appropriate (*verb*)—to assign for a specific purpose

aptly—appropriately, suitably, accurately

aquatic—belonging or living in water

arable—suitable for cultivation

arbitrary—depending solely on individual will, based on whim or impulse

arbitrate—to mediate, negotiate

arboreal—relating to trees; living in trees

arboretum—place where trees are cultivated and studied

arcane—secret, obscure, known only to a few

archaic—antiquated, from an earlier time, outdated

ardently—passionately, eagerly

ardor—great emotion or passion

arduous—demanding, strenuous, difficult

arid—extremely dry

artful—skillful in accomplishing a purpose, especially by the use of cunning or craft

articulate (*verb*)—to pronounce clearly

artifact—historical relic, item made by human craft

ascend—to rise, climb up

ascertain—to determine, discover, make certain of

ascribe—to attribute or assign (as a quality or characteristic)

ashen—resembling ashes; deathly pale

askew—crooked, tilted

assail—to attack, assault

assent (*noun*)—agreement

assert—to affirm, attest

assess—to determine the value, significance, or extent of

assimilation—act of blending in, becoming similar

assuage—to make less severe, ease, relieve

astringent—harsh, severe, stern

astute—having good judgment

asunder (*adverb*)—into different parts

atone—to make amends for a wrong

attainable—capable of being accomplished or reached

attest—to testify, stand as proof of, bear witness

audacious—bold, daring, fearless

audible—capable of being heard

augment—to increase, make greater

august—dignified, awe inspiring, majestic

authoritarian—extremely strict, bossy

auxiliary—supplementary, reserve

avail (*noun*)—use, benefit, advantage

avarice—greed

avenge—to retaliate, take revenge for an injury or crime

aver—to declare to be true, affirm

aversion—intense dislike

avert—to turn (something) away; prevent, hinder

avow—to state openly or declare

awry—crooked, askew, amiss

axiom—premise, postulate, self-evident truth

B

baleful—sinister, with evil intentions

banal—trite, overly common

bane—a source of harm or ruin

banter—playful conversation

becloud—to confuse, muddle one's perception

behemoth—huge creature

beleaguer—to harass, plague

belie—to misrepresent, give a false impression of

belittle—to speak of as unimportant, disparage, cause to seem less than another

bellicose—warlike, aggressive

belligerent—hostile, tending to fight

bellow—to roar, shout

bemused—confused, bewildered

benefactor—someone giving aid or money

beneficent—charitable; doing good deeds; producing good effects

benevolence—disposition to do good; an act of kindness

benighted—unenlightened

benign—gentle, harmless

bequeath—to give or leave through a will; to hand down

berate—to scold harshly

beseech—to beg, plead, implore

bestow—to give as a gift

betoken—to indicate, signify, give evidence of

bevy—group

blasphemous—cursing, profane, irreverent

blatant—glaring, obvious, showy

blight (*verb*)—to afflict, destroy

bovine—relating to cows; having qualities (like dullness) characteristic of cows

brazen—bold, shameless, impudent; of or like brass

breach (*noun*)—rupture, tear

broach (*verb*)—to mention for the first time; to initiate

brusque—rough and abrupt in manner

buffet (*verb*)—to toss about

buffoon—clown or fool

burly—brawny, husky

bursar—treasurer

bustle—commotion, energetic activity

byway—back road

C

cacophony—harsh sound

cadence—rhythmic flow

callous—emotionally hardened, insensitive

callow—immature, lacking sophistication

canny—smart; founded on common sense

canonize—to declare a person a saint; raise to highest honors

canvass—to conduct a poll, determine public opinion

capacious—large, roomy; extensive

capitulate—to submit completely, surrender

capricious—impulsive, whimsical, without much thought

caricature—exaggerated portrait, cartoon

cast (*verb*)—to fling, to throw

castigate—to punish, chastise, criticize severely

catalyst—something causing change without being changed

catharsis—purification, cleansing

caulk—to make watertight by sealing

causality—cause-and-effect relationship

cavort—to leap about

censorious—severely critical

cessation—temporary or complete halt

chagrin—shame, embarrassment, humiliation

charlatan—quack, fake

chastise—to punish, discipline, scold

cherubic—sweet, innocent, resembling a cherub angel

chicanery—trickery, fraud, deception

chide—to scold, express disapproval

choleric—easily angered, short-tempered

chortle—to chuckle

chronicler—one who keeps records of historical events

circumlocution—roundabout, lengthy way of saying something

circumnavigate—to bypass, go around instead of through

circumscribe—to encircle; set limits on, confine

cite—to quote as an example, to mention as proof

civility—courtesy, politeness

clairvoyant (*adj.*)—having ESP, psychic

clamor (*verb*)—to make a noisy outcry

clandestine—secretive, concealed for a darker purpose

clarity—clearness; clear understanding

claustrophobia—fear of small, confined places

clemency—merciful leniency

cloister (*verb*)—to confine, seclude

clout—power, influence

coagulate—to clot or change from a liquid to a solid

coalesce—to grow together or cause to unite as one

coerce—to compel by force or intimidation

cogent—logically forceful, compelling, convincing

cognate—related, similar, akin

coherent—intelligible, lucid, understandable

collusion—collaboration, complicity, conspiracy

comeliness—physical grace and beauty

commodious—roomy, spacious

commute—to change a penalty to a less severe one

compatriot—fellow countryman

compelled—being under moral or legal obligation, driven to do something

compensate—to repay, reimburse

complacent—self-satisfied, unconcerned

complement—to complete, make perfect

complicity—knowing partnership in wrongdoing

composure—a calmness of mind or appearance, self-possession

compunction—feeling of uneasiness caused by guilt or regret

concave—curving inward

concede—to yield, admit

conciliatory—friendly, agreeable

concur—to agree

conduit—tube, pipe, or similar passage

confection—a sweet food

conflagration—big destructive fire

confluence—meeting place; meeting of two streams

congeal—to become thick or solid, as a liquid freezing

congenial—pleasant, harmonious

conjecture—speculation, prediction

conjure—to imagine, summon (as if by magical power)

consanguineous—of the same origin; related by blood

conscientious—governed by conscience; careful and thorough

consign—to commit, entrust

console—to provide comfort or solace for a loss or hardship

constraint—something that restrains or confines

contend—to battle, clash; compete

contradict—to express the opposite of (a statement); be inconsistent with

contrite—deeply sorrowful and repentant for a wrong

contusion—bruise

convene—to meet, come together, assemble

convex—curved outward

conviction—certainty, a fixed or strong belief

convoluted—twisted, complicated, involved

copious—abundant, plentiful

coquette—woman who flirts

corporeal—having to do with the body; tangible, material

corpulence—obesity, bulkiness

correlation—association, mutual relation of two or more things (in a way not expected on the basis of chance alone)

corroborate—to confirm, verify

corrugate—to mold in a shape with parallel grooves and ridges

cosmopolitan—sophisticated, having worldwide scope

coterie—small group of people with a similar purpose

countenance (*noun*)—facial expression; look of approval or support

countervail—to counteract, exert force against

coup (*noun*)—a brilliant, sudden, and usually highly successful act or stroke

covert—hidden; secret

credible—plausible, believable

crescendo—gradual increase in volume of sound

criterion—standard for judging, rule for testing

cryptic—puzzling, mysterious

cuisine—style of cooking

culmination—climax, final stage

culpable—guilty, responsible for wrong

culprit—guilty person

curator—overseer of an exhibition, especially in an art museum

curmudgeon—cranky person

curt—abrupt, blunt

cygnet—young swan

cynic—person who distrusts the motives of others

D

daunt—to discourage, intimidate

debilitate—to weaken

debunk—to discredit, disprove

deciduous—losing leaves in the fall; short-lived, temporary

declivity—downward slope

decorum—proper behavior, etiquette

defamatory—slanderous, injurious to the reputation

defendant—person required to answer a legal action or suit

defer—to submit to the opinion or decision of another, out of respect for higher authority or knowledge

defiant—boldly resisting

defile—to disgrace, dishonor

deflect—to turn aside, especially from a straight course, deviate

deft—skillful, dexterous

déjà vu—a feeling that one has seen or heard something before

dejection—low spirits, melancholy

deleterious—harmful, destructive, detrimental

deliberate (*verb*)—to consider carefully

delta—tidal deposit at the mouth of a river

deluge (*verb*)—to submerge, overwhelm

demeanor—behavior toward others, outward manner

demystify—to remove mystery from, clarify

denigrate—to slur or blacken someone's reputation

denounce—to condemn as being evil, criticize

depict—to represent by or as if by a picture

deploy—to spread out strategically over an area

depravity—sinfulness, moral corruption

deride—to mock, ridicule, make fun of

despondent—feeling discouraged and dejected

despot—tyrannical ruler

destitute—lacking possessions and resources, suffering extreme poverty

deter—to discourage, prevent from happening

deviate—to stray, wander

devoid—totally lacking, absent of

dexterous—skilled physically or mentally

diatribe—bitter verbal attack

diffuse—to spread thinly, scatter

digression—a departure from the main subject, a turning aside of one's attention or concern

dilapidated—in disrepair, run down, neglected

diluvial—relating to a flood

diminutive—small

diplomacy—discretion, tact, skill in conducting negotiations

disbelief— refusal or reluctance to believe

discern—to perceive something obscure

disclosure—confession, admission

discordant—harsh-sounding, badly out of tune

discourse (*noun*)—conversation, discussion

discredit—to dishonor or disgrace

discrepancy—divergence or disagreement (as between facts or claims)

disengage—to disconnect, disassociate

disheveled—untidy, disarranged, unkempt

disinclination—a preference for avoiding something

dislodge—to force out of a secure or settled position

disparity—contrast, dissimilarity

dispassionate—free from emotion; impartial, unbiased

dispel—to drive out or scatter

dispense with—to suspend the operation of, do without

disperse—to break up, scatter

dispirited—disheartened, dejected

disseminate—to spread far and wide

dissipate—to gradually disperse and vanish

dissonant—harsh and unpleasant sounding

dissuade—to persuade someone to alter original intentions

distend—to swell, inflate, bloat

distraught—very worried and distressed

diurnal—daily

divert—to distract, turn off course

divine (*verb*)—to know by inspiration, intuition, or reflection

divisive—creating disunity or conflict

divulge—to reveal, make known (as a confidence)

doleful—sad, mournful

donor—benefactor, contributor

dormant—inactive, asleep

dotard—a person showing signs of senility

dour—sullen and gloomy; stern and severe

droll—amusing in a wry, subtle way

drone (*verb*)—to talk in a persistently dull or monotonous tone

dubious—questionable, unsettled in opinion, doubtful

dulcet—pleasant sounding, soothing to the ear

duly—at the expected time

dupe (*verb*)—to deceive, trick

E

ebb—to recede, decline (as the tide)

ebullient—exhilarated, full of enthusiasm and high spirits

eclectic—composed of elements drawn from various sources

eddy—air or wind current

edict—law, command, official public order

edifice—building

editorialize—to express an opinion on an issue

efficacious—effective, efficient

effluvia—outpouring of gases or vapors

effulgent—brilliantly shining

effusive—expressing emotion without restraint

egocentric—acting as if things are centered around oneself

egress (*noun*)—exit

elaborate (*verb*)—to express at greater length or in greater detail

elicit—to draw forth, bring out

eloquence—fluent and effective speech

elucidate—to give a clarifying explanation

elude—to escape the perception, understanding, or grasp of

emanate—to come or send forth, as from a source

emancipate—to set free, liberate

embellish—to adorn something with details or decoration to make it more attractive

embolden—to instill with boldness or courage

eminent—celebrated, distinguished

empathy—identification with another's feelings

emphatic—marked by emphasis, expressed forcefully

encumber—to hinder, burden, restrict motion

endurance—ability to withstand hardships

enervate—to weaken, sap strength from

engaged—greatly interested, involved in activity

engender—to produce, cause, bring about

enigma—a mystery; something inexplicable

enjoin—to direct with authority and emphasis

enmity—hostility, antagonism, ill-will

ennui—boredom, lack of interest and energy

ensconce—to settle comfortably into a place

enshroud—to cover, enclose with a dark cover

enthrall—to captivate, enchant, hold spellbound

entity—something with its own existence or form

entreat—to plead, beg

entrepreneur—one who organizes and assumes the risks of a business or enterprise

enunciate—to pronounce clearly

ephemeral—momentary, transient, fleeting

equanimity—calmness, composure

equestrian—relating to horseback riding

errant—straying, mistaken, roving

erratic—eccentric, strange, lacking consistency

eschew—to abstain from, avoid

estrange—to alienate, cause a break in affection

ethereal—not earthly, spiritual, delicate

ethos—beliefs or character of a group

eurythmics—art of harmonious bodily movement

evade—to avoid, slip away

evasiveness—deliberate vagueness or ambiguity

evince—to show clearly, display, signify

exasperation—irritation, aggravation

excerpt (*noun*)—selection from a book or play

excruciating—agonizing, intensely painful

exhaust (*verb*)—to use up completely, deplete

exhort—to urge or incite by strong appeals

exhume—to remove from a grave

exonerate—to clear of blame, absolve

expansive—sweeping, comprehensive

expedite—to accelerate the process of, speed up

exploit (*verb*)—to use to one's advantage

expound—to elaborate; to expand or increase

expunge—to erase, eliminate completely

extol—to praise

extremity—outermost or farthest point

extricate—to free from, disentangle

exuberant—lively, enthusiastic

exude—to give off, ooze

F

fabricated—constructed, invented; faked, falsified

façade—face, front; mask, superficial appearance

facile—very easy, achieved with little work

fallacious—wrong, unsound, tending to mislead

fallow—uncultivated, unused

farcical—absurd, ludicrous

fathom (*verb*)—to measure the depth of, gauge

fecund—fertile, fruitful, productive

feeble—weak, lacking in strength

feign—to pretend, give a false impression

fervor—intensity of feeling or expression

fetid—foul-smelling, putrid

fetter—to bind, chain, confine

fitful—intermittent, irregular

flammable—capable of burning rapidly

flippant—lacking proper respect or seriousness

flora—plants

fodder—raw material, as for artistic creation

foible—minor weakness or character flaw

foment—to arouse, incite

foreboding—dark sense of evil to come

forethought—anticipation, foresight

forlorn—dreary, unhappy; hopeless, despairing

formidable—extremely impressive in strength or excellence; inspiring fear

formulate—to conceive, draft, plan

forsaken—abandoned

forte—one's strong point, talent

founder (*verb*)—to fall helplessly; sink

fracas—noisy dispute

frankness—honest and straightforward expression

fraud—cheat, imposter

frenzied—feverishly fast, hectic, and confused

frivolous—petty, trivial; flippant, silly

furtive—secret, stealthy

fusion—process of merging things into one

futile—completely ineffective, useless

G

gait—manner of walking

garrulous—very talkative

gaunt—thin and bony

gavel—mallet used for commanding attention

genre—type, class, category

gibe (*noun*)—an expression of sarcastic scorn

gingerly—cautiously, carefully

girth—distance around something

glib—offhand, casual

glower—to glare, stare angrily and intensely

gluttony—eating and drinking to excess

gnarled—knotted, soured in character

goad—to prod or urge

grandiose—magnificent and imposing; exaggerated and pretentious

granular—having a grainy texture

gratis—free, costing nothing

gratuity—something given voluntarily, tip

grievous—causing grief or sorrow; serious and distressing

grimace (*verb*)—to make a facial expression showing pain or disgust

grimy—dirty, filthy

gullible—easily deceived

gustatory—relating to sense of taste

H

habitat—dwelling place

hackneyed—worn out by overuse

hamlet—small village

harbinger—precursor, sign of something to come

hardy—robust, vigorous

harrowing—extremely distressing, terrifying

haughty—arrogant and condescending

heinous—shocking, wicked, terrible

hemorrhage (*verb*)—to bleed heavily

hiatus—break, interruption, vacation

hinterland—wilderness

husband (*verb*)—to farm

hydrate—to add water to

hyperbole—purposeful exaggeration for effect

hyperventilate—to breathe abnormally fast

hypothesis—assumption subject to proof

hypothetical—theoretical, speculative

I

iconoclast—one who attacks traditional beliefs

idle—inactive, not in use

ignoble—dishonorable, not noble in character

ilk—type or kind

illicit—illegal, improper

imbue—to saturate or invade as if by dyeing

immerse—to engross, preoccupy

immobile—not moveable; still

impartial—not biased, not favoring one more than another

impasse—blocked path, dilemma with no solution

impeccable—flawless, without fault

impertinent—rude, exceeding the bounds of good taste

impetuous—quick to act without thinking

implausible—improbable, inconceivable

implicit—implied, not directly expressed

imposing—dignified, grand

impotent—powerless, ineffective, lacking strength

impromptu—spontaneous, without rehearsal

impropriety—an improper act

impudent—arrogant, audacious

impulse—sudden tendency, inclination

inadvertently—unintentionally

incandescent—shining brightly, glowing

incapacitate—to disable, deprive of capacity

incarnadine—blood-red in color

incarnate—having bodily form

incense (*verb*)—to infuriate, enrage

inception—beginning

incessant—continuous, never ceasing

inclination—a tendency toward a certain condition or character

inconceivable—impossible, unthinkable

inconsequential—unimportant, trivial

incredulous—skeptical, doubtful

incriminating—showing evidence of involvement in a crime or fault

inculcate—to teach, impress in the mind

incursion—sudden invasion

indefatigable—never tired

indicative—showing or pointing out, suggestive of

indict—to accuse formally, charge with a crime

indigenous—native, occurring naturally in an area

indignant—angry, incensed, offended

industry—business or trade

inebriated—drunk, intoxicated

inept—clumsy, awkward

inevitable—certain, unavoidable

inexorable—inflexible, unyielding, relentless

inextricable—incapable of being disentangled

infer—to conclude, deduce

infiltrate—to pass secretly into enemy territory

infuriate—to anger, provoke, outrage

ingress—entrance

inimical—hostile, unfriendly

iniquity—sin, evil act

inkling—hint; vague idea

innate—natural, existing in an individual from birth

innocuous—harmless, inoffensive

innuendo—indirect and subtle criticism, insinuation

innumerable—too many to be counted

inoffensive—harmless, innocent

inopportune—badly timed, inappropriate

inquest—investigation; court or legal proceeding

insidious—sly, treacherous, developing slowly before becoming apparent

insinuate—to subtly and indirectly suggest, hint

instigate—to incite, urge, agitate

insular—characteristic of an isolated people; having a narrow, provincial viewpoint

integral—central, indispensable

integrity—decency, honesty; wholeness

interject—to interpose, insert

interloper—trespasser; meddler in others' affairs

interminable—endless

intermittent—starting and stopping

intimation—clue, suggestion

intrepid—fearless

inundate—to cover with water; overwhelm

invective—an abusive expression or speech

invidious—tending to cause discontent

invoke—to call upon, conjure

irascible—easily angered

ironic—humorous, as a result of something being contrary to what was expected

irrevocably—conclusively, irreversibly

J

jaded—dulled by excess or overuse; slightly cynical

jettison—to cast off, discard

jocular—jovial, playful, humorous

jubilee—special anniversary

juggernaut—huge force destroying everything in its path

juncture—point where two things are joined

juxtaposition—the placement of two or more things side by side

K

keen (*adj.*)—having a sharp edge; intellectually sharp, perceptive

kernel—essential part, grain

keynote—note or tone on which a musical key is founded; theme or idea of a speech, etc.

kindle—to set fire to; excite or inspire

kudos—fame, glory, honor

L

labyrinth—maze

laceration—cut, wound

lachrymose—tearful

lackadaisical—idle, lazy; apathetic, indifferent

laconic—using few words

laggard—dawdler, loafer, lazy person

lament (*verb*)—to express grief for, mourn

lampoon—to attack with satire, mock harshly

languid—lacking energy, indifferent, slow

lap (*verb*)—to wash against

largess—generosity; gift

larynx—organ containing vocal cords

latent—present but hidden

leery—suspicious

legible—capable of being read

legislate—to make or enact laws

levity—humor, frivolity, lightheartedness

liberal—tolerant, broad-minded

limpid—transparently clear, simple; calm, serene

lineage—ancestry

lionize—to treat as a celebrity, regard with great interest

listless—lacking energy and enthusiasm

lithe—readily bent, gracefully flexible

livid—reddened with anger

loath—reluctant

loathe—to abhor, despise, hate

locomotion—movement from place to place

logo—identifying symbol, motto

loiter—to stand around idly with no obvious purpose

low (*verb*)—to make a sound like a cow, moo

lucid—clear and easily understood

lugubrious—sorrowful, mournful; dismal

lumber (*verb*)—to move slowly and awkwardly

luminous—bright, brilliant, glowing

lunar—relating to the moon

lurid—shocking, sensational, melodramatic

lurk—to lie hidden, especially for an evil purpose

M

machination—a scheming or crafty action intended to bring about an often evil result

maelstrom—whirlpool, turmoil

magnanimous—generous, noble in spirit

magnate—powerful or influential person

magnitude—extent, greatness of size

malediction—curse

malefactor—evil-doer; culprit

malevolent—ill-willed; causing evil or harm to others

malice—deep-seated hatred, desire to cause distress or pain to another

malodorous—foul smelling

manifest (*verb*)—to show plainly, reveal

maritime—relating to the sea or sailing

masochistic—enjoying pain or humiliation

matriculate—to enroll as a member of a college or university

matrilineal—tracing ancestry through mother's line rather than father's

meritorious—deserving reward or praise

metaphor—figure of speech comparing two different things

meticulously—carefully, painstakingly

mettle—courage, endurance, spirit

minuscule—very small

mirth—frivolity, gaiety, laughter

mishap—accident; misfortune

missive—note or letter

mitigate—to soften, make milder

mock—to ridicule, laugh scorningly at

mollify—to calm, make less severe

mollusk—sea animal with soft body

monochromatic—having one color

montage—a single composition made up of several pictures or designs

morbid—gruesome; relating to disease; abnormally gloomy

mores—customs or manners

morose—broodingly unhappy

mote—small particle, speck

mundane—worldly; commonplace

munificent—generous

muse (*verb*)—to wonder about

myopic—nearsighted; unable to think in the long term, narrowly seen

myriad—immense number, multitude

N

nadir—lowest point

natal—relating to birth

nebulous—vague, cloudy

nefarious—wicked, evil

nemesis—a source of harm or ruin; a strong opponent or rival

neophyte—novice, beginner

niche—recess in a wall; an area well suited to something

noisome—stinking, putrid

nomadic—moving from place to place

nonchalantly—with an air of easy unconcern, indifferently

notoriety—unfavorable fame

novel (*adj.*)—new, striking

novice—apprentice, beginner

noxious—harmful, distasteful

numismatics—coin collecting

O

obdurately—stubbornly, inflexibly

obfuscate—to confuse, obscure

oblige—to do something as or as if a favor

obliterate—to demolish, wipe out

oblivious—unaware, inattentive

obscurity—darkness, absence of light

obsequious—overly submissive and obedient, fawning over

obsolete—no longer in use

obstinate—stubborn

occlude—to shut, block

odious—hateful, contemptible

ominous—menacing, threatening, indicating misfortune

onerous—burdensome, troublesome

opaque—impervious to light; difficult to understand

operative (*adj.*)—functioning, working

opine—to express an opinion

opportunist—one who takes advantage of circumstances, often unethically

opulence—wealth (often in a showy manner)

oration—lecture, formal speech

orb—spherical body

ornate—elaborately decorated, highly ornamented

ostentatious—showy

ostracism—exclusion, temporary banishment

outspoken—unreserved in speech, blunt

P

pacific—calm, peaceful

palatial—like a palace, magnificent

palaver—idle talk

palette—board for mixing paints; range of colors

pallor—paleness, lack of (facial) color

palpable—obvious, real, tangible

palpitation—throbbing, rapid beating

paltry—pitifully small or worthless

panoply—impressive array

panorama—broad view; comprehensive picture

paradoxical—seemingly contradictory, incongruous

paragon—model of excellence or perfection

parameters—limits, boundaries; characteristics

paramount—supreme, dominant, primary

parched (*adj.*)—dry, thirsty

pariah—outcast

parochial—of limited scope or outlook, provincial

parry—to avoid, turn aside, deflect

patent (*noun*)—official document giving exclusive right to sell an invention

paternity—fatherhood; descent from father's ancestors

patrician (*adj.*)—aristocratic

patronize—to condescend to, disparage; to buy from

paucity—scarcity, lack

pavilion—tent or light building used for shelter or exhibitions

peccadillo—minor sin or offense

pedant—a formalist in teaching, one who stresses the trivial in learning

pedestrian (*adj.*)—commonplace, undistinguished, ordinary

pediment—triangular gable on a roof or facade

peer (*noun*)—someone who is of equal standing, a contemporary

pejorative—having bad connotations, disparaging, belittling

penance—voluntary suffering to repent for a wrong

penchant—inclination, a liking toward something

penultimate—next to last

perambulator—baby carriage

pernicious—highly destructive

perpetual—endless, lasting

perplexed—puzzled, confused

pertinent—applicable, appropriate

peruse—to examine closely

phalanx—massed group of people, animals, or things

phenomenon—a rare and unaccountable fact or occurrence, a marvel

philanderer—pursuer of casual love affairs

philanthropy—love of humanity; generosity to worthy causes

phobia—exaggerated, illogical fear

pinnacle—peak, highest point of development

pique (*noun*)—fleeting feeling of hurt pride, resentment

pithy—profound, substantial; concise, succinct, to the point

pittance—meager amount or wage

placate—to soothe, pacify

placid—calm

plaintive—melancholy, expressing sorrow

plausible—seemingly valid, likely, or acceptable; credible

plethora—excess, overabundance

ploy—a calculating plan, a maneuver that will achieve an intended result

plucky—courageous, spunky

plummet—to fall, plunge

podium—platform or lectern for orchestra conductors or speakers

poignant—emotionally moving

ponder—to consider, think about

pore (*verb*)—to study closely or meditatively

porous—full of holes, permeable to liquids

portent—omen

portly—stout, dignified

portrayal—a representation by picture or drawing

posterity—future generations; all of a person's descendants

potable—drinkable

potent—powerful, strong; having a strong effect

prattle (*noun*)—meaningless, foolish talk

precarious—dependent on uncertain conditions

precede—to come ahead or in front of; to be earlier than

preclude—to rule out

precursor—forerunner, predecessor

predator—one that preys on others, destroyer

predicament—difficult situation

predisposition—tendency, disposition in advance to behave in a certain way

preposterous—absurd, illogical

presage—to foretell, indicate in advance

prescient—having foresight

prevalent—widespread

prevaricate—to lie, evade the truth

primordial—original, existing from the beginning

pristine—untouched, uncorrupted

proclaim—to declare, announce

proclivity—tendency, inclination

procrastinator—one who continually and unjustifiably postpoₛ

proficient—expert, skilled in a certain subject

progenitor—originator, forefather, ancestor in a direct line

progeny—offspring, future generations

propinquity—nearness

proponent—advocate, defender, supporter

prostrate (*adj.*)—lying face downward

protrusion—something that sticks out

provincial—rustic, unsophisticated, limited in scope

prowess—bravery, skill

pry—to intrude into; force open

pseudonym—pen name; fictitious or borrowed name

psychic (*adj.*)—perceptive of nonmaterial, spiritual forces

pudgy—chubby, overweight

pugnacious—quarrelsome, eager and ready to fight

pulchritude—beauty

pungent—strong or sharp in smell or taste

purport—to profess, suppose, claim

Q

quadrilateral—four-sided polygon

quagmire—difficult situation, predicament

qualify—to provide with needed skills; modify, limit

quandary—dilemma, difficulty

quash (*verb*)—to put down, extinguish completely

quaternary—consisting of or relating to four units or members

quell—to crush, subdue

querulous—inclined to complain, irritable

query (*noun*)—question

quiver—to shake slightly, tremble, vibrate

quixotic—overly idealistic, impractical

R

rally (*verb*)—to assemble in support

ramble—to roam, wander; to babble, digress

ramification—an implication, outgrowth, or consequence

rancid—offensive in smell or taste

rant—to harangue, rave, forcefully scold

rapt—deeply absorbed

rash (*adj.*)—careless, hasty, reckless

rationalize—to think of self-satisfying but incorrect reasons for
one's behavior

raucous—harsh sounding, boisterous

ravine—deep, narrow gorge

raze—to tear down, demolish

reactionary—marked by extreme conservatism, especially in politics

rebuff (*verb*)—to reject or criticize sharply; snub

rebuke—to reprimand, scold

rebut—to refute by evidence or argument

recalcitrant—resisting authority or control

recant—to retract a statement or opinion

recede—to move back or away from a limit or point

reclusive—shut off from the world

recoil—to shrink back, as in fear

recount—to describe facts or events

recurring—repeating

refectory—room where meals are served

refract—to deflect sound or light

refuge—escape, shelter

refurbish—to renovate

refute—to contradict, discredit

regimen—government rule; systematic plan

reiterate—to say or do again, repeat

rejuvenate—to make young again; renew

relegate—to refer or assign for decision or action

relish (*verb*)—to enjoy greatly

reminiscent—tending to recall or suggest something in the past

remote—distant, isolated

remuneration—pay or reward for work or goods

repentant—apologetic, guilty, remorseful

repudiate—to reject as having no authority

requisite (*adj.*)—required by the nature of things or by circumstances

resolute (*adj.*)—firm or determined; unwavering; with a clear purpose

resolve (*verb*)—to conclude, determine

resonate—to call forth a feeling of shared emotion or belief

resort (*verb*)—to fall back on something in a time of need

respite—interval of relief

restive—impatient, uneasy, restless

reticent—not speaking freely; reserved

retiring—shy, modest, reserved

retort (*verb*)—to answer back in a sharp manner

retract—to take back

retrieve—to bring, fetch; reclaim

revelry—boisterous festivity

revere—to worship, regard with awe

revert—to backslide, regress

rife—widespread; abounding

riveted—fastened firmly; engrossed

rococo—very highly ornamented

rostrum—stage for public speaking

rotund—round in shape; fat

rue—to regret

ruminate—to contemplate, reflect upon

ruthless—having no compassion or pity, merciless

S

sacrosanct—extremely sacred, beyond criticism

sagacious—wise, insightful, perceptive

salutation—greeting

sanctuary—haven, retreat

sardonic—skeptically humorous, sarcastic

saunter—to walk about in a leisurely manner, stroll

savory—agreeable in taste or smell

scale (*verb*)—to climb to the top of

scenario—plot outline; possible situation

scoff—to treat with disrespect and scorn, ridicule

scrutiny—careful observation

secluded—isolated, remote

sensibility—refined sensitivity to matters of feeling or changes in the environment

serenity—calm, peacefulness

serpentine—serpent-like; twisting, winding

serrated—saw-toothed, notched

shard—piece of broken glass or pottery

sheepish—timid, meek, or bashful due to self-consciousness

shrill (*adj.*)—having a sharp, high-pitched sound, piecing

sinuous—winding; intricate, complex

skeptical—doubtful, questioning

skulk—to move in a secretive manner, sneak, lurk

smug—highly self-satisfied

sobriquet—nickname

sojourn—visit, stay

solace—comfort in distress; consolation

solarium—room or glassed-in area exposed to the sun

solidarity—unity based on common aims or interests

somnolent—drowsy, sleepy; inducing sleep

sonorous—producing a full, rich sound

sordid—filthy; contemptible and corrupt

spartan—simple, bare

spawn—to generate, produce

speculate—to contemplate, wonder

sportive—frolicsome, playful

spur (*verb*)—to prod

spurn—to reject or refuse contemptuously; scorn

squalid—filthy, rundown

staccato—marked by abrupt, clear-cut sounds

stagnant—stale, not flowing or developing

staid—self-restrained to the point of dullness

stasis—motionless state; standstill

stilted—stiff, unnatural

stoic—indifferent to or unaffected by emotions

stolid—having or showing little emotion

stylize—to fashion, formalize

stymie—to block, thwart

suave—smoothly polite, superficially gracious

subdued—suppressed, stifled

subliminal—subconscious, imperceptible, existing below the threshold of consciousness

subsequent—following in time or order

subside—to settle down, decrease

subterranean—hidden, secret; underground

subtle—refined, marked by keen insight

succession—sequence, series

succulent—juicy; full of vitality or freshness

sullen—brooding, gloomy

sully—to stain, tarnish, defile

sundry—various, miscellaneous

superfluous—exceeding what is sufficient or necessary

supplant—to replace, substitute

suppress—to restrain from a usual course or action

surfeit—an excess, oversupply

surly—rude and bad-tempered

surmise—to make an educated guess

surplus—excess

surreal—having an oddly dreamlike quality

surreptitiously—secretly

suspect (*adj.*)—suspected; doubtful, questionable

sustain—to support, uphold; endure

symposium—meeting with short presentations on related topics

T

tableaux—vivid descriptions, striking scenes

tacit—silently understood or implied

talon—claw of an animal, especially a bird of prey

tangible—able to be sensed, perceptible, measurable

tattered—torn into shreds, ragged

tempered—moderated, restrained

tenet—belief, doctrine

tentative—not fully worked out, uncertain; hesitant

tenuous—weak, insubstantial

tepid—lukewarm; showing little enthusiasm

terse—concise, brief, free of extra words

testament—statement of belief; will

tether—to bind, tie

thwart—to block or prevent from happening; frustrate

tidings—news

timorous—timid, shy, full of apprehension

tirade—long, violent speech; verbal assault

titan—person of colossal stature or achievement

tome—book, usually large and academic

tonal—relating to pitch or sound

torsion—act of twisting and turning

totter—to sway as if about to fall

toxin—poison

transcription—copy, reproduction; record

translucent—partially transparent

tremulous—trembling, nervous, shaky

trepidation—fear, apprehension

troupe—a group of actors

tryst—agreement between lovers to meet; rendezvous

tyro—beginner, novice

U

unadulterated—absolutely pure

unctuous—greasy, oily; smug and falsely earnest

undermine—to sabotage, weaken secretly and gradually

undulate—to give a wavelike appearance

unheralded—unannounced, unexpected, not publicized

unkempt—uncombed, messy in appearance

unwarranted—groundless, unjustified

unwitting—unconscious; unintentional

unyielding—firm, resolute

upbraid—to scold sharply

urbane—courteous, refined, suave

utilitarian—efficient, functional, useful

utopia—perfect place

V

vanquish—to conquer, defeat

variegated—varied; marked with different colors

vaunted—boasted about, bragged about

vehemently—intensely, forcefully

veracity—accuracy, truth

verbatim—word for word

verbose—wordy

verdant—green with vegetation

vernal—related to spring

vestige—trace, remnant

vex—to irritate, annoy; confuse, puzzle

viable—workable, able to succeed or grow

vie—to strive for superiority, compete

vigilant—attentive, watchful

vilify—to slander, defame

vim—energy, enthusiasm

vindicate—to clear of suspicion or blame, justify or prove the worth of (especially in light of later developments)

vindictive—spiteful, vengeful, unforgiving

virulent—extremely poisonous; malignant; hateful

viscous—thick, syrupy, sticky

vivid—bright and intense in color; strongly perceived

vociferous—loud, vocal, and noisy

void (*noun*)—emptiness, vacuum

volley (*noun*)—flight of missiles, round of gunshots

voluminous—large, having great volume

voracious—having a great appetite

vulnerable—defenseless, unprotected; innocent, naive

W

wallow—to indulge oneself excessively, luxuriate

wan—sickly pale, lacking vitality

wary—mistrustful, on guard, cautious

wayward—erratic, unrestrained, reckless

weather (*verb*)—to endure, undergo

wield—to handle

wily—clever, deceptive

wrath (*noun*)—strong vindictive anger

writ—written document, usually in law

writhe—to twist, as in pain, struggle, or embarrassment

wry—amusing, ironic

X

xenophobia—fear or hatred of foreigners or strangers

Y

yen—a strong desire; a craving

Z

zeal—eagerness, enthusiasm, passion

zealot—someone passionately devoted to a cause

zenith—highest point, summit

zephyr—gentle breeze

ROOT LIST

A, AN
not, without
amoral, asymmetrical, anesthetic, anonymity

AB, A
from, away, apart
abnormal, aberration, abscond, annul, aversion

AC, ACR
sharp, sour
acid, acerbic, exacerbate, acute, acuity, acumen, acrid, acrimony

AD, A
to, toward
adhere, adjacent, adjunct, admonish, adroit, aspire, attest

ALI, ALTR
another
alias, alienate, inalienable, altruism

APPENDIXES

AM, AMI
love
amorous, amicable, amiable, amity

AMBI, AMPHI
both
ambiguous, ambivalent, ambidextrous, amphibious

AMBL, AMBUL
walk
amble, ambulatory

ANIM
mind, spirit, breath
animosity, unanimous, magnanimous

ANN, ENN
year
annual, annuity, perennial

ANTE, ANT
before
antecedent, antiquated, anticipate

ANTHROP
human
anthropology, anthropomorphic, misanthrope, philanthropy

ANTI, ANT
against, opposite
antidote, antipathy, antithesis, antacid, antagonist, antonym

AUD
hear
audio, audience, audition, auditory, audible

AUTO
self
autobiography, autocrat, autonomous

BELLI, BELL
war
belligerent, bellicose, antebellum, rebellion

BENE, BEN
good
benevolent, benefactor, beneficent, benign

BI
two
bicycle, bisect, bilateral, bilingual, biped

BIBLIO
book
Bible, bibliography, bibliophile

BIO
life
biography, biology, amphibious, symbiotic

BURS
money, purse
reimburse, disburse, bursar

CAD, CAS, CID
happen, fall
accident, cadence, cascade, deciduous

CAP, CIP
head
captain, decapitate, capitulate, precipitous, precipitate, recapitulate

CARN
flesh
carnal, carnage, carnival, carnivorous, incarnate

CAP, CAPT, CEPT, CIP
take, hold, seize
capable, captivate, deception, intercept, inception, anticipate, emancipation

CED, CESS
yield, go
cease, incessant, precede, recede, antecedent

CHROM
color
chrome, chromatic, monochrome

CHRON
time
chronology, chronic, anachronism

CIDE
murder
homicide, suicide

CIRCUM
around
circumference, circumscribe, circumspect, circumvent

CLIN, CLIV
slope
incline, declivity, proclivity

CLUD, CLUS, CLAUS, CLOIS
shut, close
conclude, reclusive, claustrophobia

CO, COM, CON
with, together
coerce, cogent, compassion, condone, consensus, constrained, contentious, convene

COGN, GNO
know
recognize, incognito, diagnosis, agnostic, prognosis, ignorant

CONTRA
against
controversy, incontrovertible, contravene

CORP
body
corpse, corporeal, corpulence

COSMO, COSM
world
cosmopolitan, cosmos, microcosm, macrocosm

CRAC, CRAT
rule, power
democracy, bureaucracy, autocrat, aristocrat

CRED
trust, believe
incredible, credulous, credence

CRESC, CRET
grow
crescent, crescendo

CULP
blame, fault
culprit, culpable, inculpate

CURR, CURS
run
current, concur, cursory, precursor, incursion

DE
down, out, apart
depart, debilitate, defamatory, defunct, delegate, deprecate, devoid

DEC
ten, tenth
decade, decimal, decathlon, decimate

DEMO, DEM
people
democrat, demographics, epidemic

DI, DIURN
day
diary, quotidian, diurnal

DIA
across
diagonal, diatribe, diaphanous

DIC, DICT
speak
diction, predict, indict, verdict

DIS, DIF, DI
not, apart, away
discern, discord, discredit, disseminate, differentiate, diffidence, digress, divert

DOC, DOCT
teach
docile, doctrine, doctrinaire

DOL
pain
condolence, doleful, dolorous, indolent

DUC, DUCT
lead
seduce, induce, conduct, induct

EGO
self
ego, egoist, egocentric

EN, EM
in, into
enter, entice, ensconce, enthrall, embellish, embroil, empathy

ERR
wander
erratic, aberration, errant

EU
well, good
eulogy, euphemism, euphony, euphoria, eurythmics, euthanasia

EX, E
out, out of
exit, exacerbate, excerpt, excommunicate, expedient, extenuating, extremity, evict, elicit

FAC, FIC, FECT, FY, FEA
make, do
factory, benefactor, beneficent, affect, confection, magnify, unify

FAL, FALS
deceive
infallible, fallacious, false

FERV
boil
fervent, fervid, effervescent

FID
faith, trust
confident, diffidence, fidelity

FLU, FLUX
flow
fluent, affluent, superfluous, flux

FORE
before
forecast, foreboding

FRAG, FRAC
break
fragment, fracture, fractious, refract

FUS
pour
profuse, infusion, effusive

GEN
birth, class, kin
generation, congenital, homogeneous, heterogeneous, ingenious

GRAD, GRESS
step
graduate, gradual, centigrade, progress, digress, transgress

GRAPH, GRAM
writing
biography, bibliography, grammar

GRAT
pleasing
grateful, gratitude, gratis, gratuitous, gratuity

GRAV, GRIEV
heavy
grave, gravity, aggravate, grieve, grievous

GREG
crowd, flock
gregarious, egregious, congregate, aggregate

HABIT, HIBIT
have, hold
habit, cohabit, habitat, inhibit

HAP
by chance
happen, haphazard, mishap

HELIO, HELI
sun
heliocentric, heliotrope, helium

HETERO
other
heterogeneous

HOL
whole
holocaust, catholic, holistic

HOMO
same
homogenize, homogeneous, homonym

HOMO
man
homo sapiens, homicide

HYDR
water
hydrant, hydrate, dehydration

HYPER
too much, excess
hyperactive, hyperbole, hyperventilate

HYPO
too little, under
hypothermia, hypochondria, hypothesis, hypothetical

IN, IG, IL, IM, IR
not
indefatigable, inept, insatiable, insomnia, incessant, insipid, impasse, impervious

IN, IL, IM, IR
in, on, into
invade, inaugurate, introvert, infer, insinuate, implicate

INTER
between, among
intercept, intermittent, interrogate, intervene

INTRA, INTR
within
intravenous, intramural, intrinsic

IT, ITER
between, among
transit, itinerant, transitory, reiterate

JECT, JET
throw
interject, abject, trajectory, jettison

JOUR
day
journal, adjourn, sojourn

JUD
judge
judicious, prejudice, adjudicate

JUNCT, JUG
join
junction, adjunct, injunction, subjugate

JUR
swear, law
jury, abjure, conjure, perjure, jurisprudence

LAT
side
lateral, collateral, unilateral, bilateral, quadrilateral

LAV, LAU, LU
wash
lavatory, laundry, ablution

LEG, LEC, LEX
read, speak
legible, lecture, lexicon

LEV
light
levitate, levity, alleviate

LIBER
free
liberal, libertarian, libertine

LIG, LECT
choose, gather
eligible, select

LIG, LI
bind
ligament, oblige, religion, liable, liaison

LING, LANG
tongue
linguistics, bilingual

LITER
letter
literate, alliteration, literal

LITH
stone
monolith, lithograph, megalith

LOQU, LOC, LOG
speech, thought
eloquent, loquacious, colloquial, soliloquy, circumlocution, interlocutor, eulogy

LUC, LUM
light
lucid, elucidate, translucent, illuminate

LUD, LUS
play
ludicrous, allude, delusion, allusion, illusory

MACRO
great
macrocosm, macrobiotics

MAG, MAJ, MAS, MAX
great
magnanimous, magnitude, majesty

MAL
bad
malady, maladroit, malevolent

MAN
hand
emancipate, manifest

MAR
sea
marine, maritime

MATER, MATR
mother
maternal, matron, matrilineal

MEDI
middle
intermediary, medieval, mediate

MEGA
great
megaphone, megalomania, megalith

MEM, MEN
remember
memento, memorabilia, reminisce

METER, METR, MENS
measure
thermometer, perimeter, metronome, commensurate

MICRO
small
microscope, microorganism, microcosm, microbe

MIS
wrong, bad, hate
misanthrope, misconstrue, misnomer

MIT, MISS
send
emit, missive

MOLL
soft
mollify, emollient, mollusk

MON, MONIT
warn
admonish, monitor, premonition

MONO
one
monologue, monotonous, monogamy, monolith, monochrome

MOR
custom, manner
moral, mores, morose

MOR, MORT
dead
morbid, moribund, mortal, amortize

MORPH
shape
amorphous, anthropomorphic, metamorphosis

MOV, MOT, MOB, MOM
move
mobile, momentum, momentous

MUT
change
mutate, mutability, immutable

NAT, NASC
born
natal, neonate, innate, cognate, nascent, renaissance

NAU, NAV
ship, sailor
nautical, circumnavigate

NEG
not, deny
abnegate, renege

NEO
new
neoclassical, neophyte, neologism, neonate

NIHIL
none, nothing
annihilation, nihilism

NOM, NYM
name
nomenclature, nominal, misnomer, anonymity

NOX, NIC, NEC, NOC
harm
noxious, pernicious, internecine, innocuous

NOV
new
novelty, innovation, novitiate

NUMER
number
numeral, numerous, innumerable, enumerate

OB
against
obdurate, obfuscate, obsequious, obstinate, obstreperous

OMNI
all
omnipresent, omniscient, omnivorous

ONER
burden
onerous, exonerate

OPER
work
cooperate, inoperable

PAC
peace
pacifist, pacific

PALP
feel
palpable, palpitation

PAN
all
panorama, panacea, pandemic

PATER, PATR
father
paternal, expatriate, patrician

PATH, PASS
feel, suffer
antipathy, empathy, apathy, pathos, impassioned

PEC
money
pecuniary, impecunious

PED, POD
foot
pedestrian, pediment, expedient, biped, quadruped, tripod

PEL, PULS
drive
compel, compelling, expel, propel, compulsion

PEN
almost
peninsula, penultimate, penumbra

PEND, PENS
hang
pendant, pendulous, compendium, suspense, propensity

PER
through, by, for, throughout
perfunctory, permeable, perspicacious, pertinacious, perusal

PER
against, destruction
perfidious, pernicious, perjure

PERI
around
perimeter, periphery, peripatetic

PET
seek, go toward
petition, impetus, impetuous, petulant

PHIL
love
philanthropy, bibliophile, philology

PHOB
fear
claustrophobia, xenophobia

PHON
sound
phonetics, phonics

PLAC
calm, please
placate, implacable, placid, complacent

PON, POS
put, place
proponent, exponent, posit, interpose, juxtaposition, depose

PORT
carry
portable, deportment, rapport

POT
drink
potion, potable

POT
power
potent, potentate, omnipotence

PRE
before
precede, precipitate, predisposition, preponderance, premonition

PRIM, PRI
first
primal, primeval, primordial, pristine

PRO
ahead, forth
proclivity, profuse, prognosis, prologue, proponent

PROTO
first
prototype, protagonist, protocol

PROX, PROP
near
approximate, proximity, propinquity

PSEUDO
false
pseudoscientific, pseudonym

PYR
fire
pyromania

QUAD, QUAR, QUAT
four
quadrilateral, quadrant, quadruped

QUES, QUER, QUIS, QUIR
question
quest, inquest, query, querulous, inquisitive, inquiry

QUIE
quiet
acquiesce

QUINT, QUIN
five
quintuplets, quintessence

RADI, RAMI
branch
radius, radiate, eradicate, ramification

RECT, REG
straight, rule
rectangle, rectitude, rectify

REG
king, rule
regent, interregnum

RETRO
backward
retrospective, retroactive, retrograde

RID, RIS
laugh
deride, derision

ROG
ask
derogatory, abrogate, arrogate

RUD
rough, crude
rude, erudite, rudimentary

RUPT
break
disrupt, interrupt, rupture

SACR, SANCT
holy
sacrilege, consecrate, sanctify, sanction, sacrosanct

SCRIB, SCRIPT, SCRIV
write
ascribe, circumscribe, inscribe, proscribe

SE
apart, away
segregate, secede, sedition

SEC, SECT, SEG
cut
sector, dissect, segment, secant

SED, SID
sit
sedate, sedentary, supersede, insidious

SEM
seed, sow
seminal, disseminate

SEN
old
senile, senescent

SENT, SENS
feel, think
assent, sentient, consensus

SEQU, SECU
follow
obsequious, non sequitur

SIM, SEM
similar, same
verisimilitude, semblance, dissemble

SIGN
mark, sign
designation, assignation

SIN
curve
sine curve, sinuous, insinuate

SOL
sun
solar, parasol, solarium, solstice

SOL
alone
solo, solitude, soliloquy, solipsism

SOMN
sleep
insomnia, somnolent, somnambulist

SON
sound
sonic, consonance, dissonance, assonance, sonorous, resonate

SOPH
wisdom
philosopher, sophistry, sophomoric

SPEC, SPIC
see, look
circumspect, retrospective, perspicacious, perspicuous

SPER
hope
prosper, prosperous, despair, desperate

SPERS, SPAR
scatter
disperse, sparse, aspersion, disparate

SPIR
breathe
respire, inspire, spiritual, aspire, transpire

STRICT, STRING
bind
constrict, stringent, astringent

STRUCT, STRU
build
structure, obstruct, construe

SUB
under
subjugate, subliminal, subterranean, subvert

SUMM
highest
summit, summary, consummate

SUPER, SUR
above
supervise, supercilious, supersede, insurmountable, surfeit

SURGE, SURRECT
rise
surge, resurgent, insurgent, insurrection

SYN, SYM
together
synthesis, synopsis, symposium, symbiosis

TACIT, TIC
silent
tacit, taciturn, reticent

TACT, TAG, TANG
touch
tactile, contagious, tangent, tangible

TEN, TIN, TAIN
hold, twist
detention, tenable, tenacious, pertinacious, retinue, retain

TEND, TENS, TENT
stretch
distend, tension, ostensible, contentious

TERM
end
terminal, terminus, interminable

TERR
earth, land
terrestrial, extraterrestrial, subterranean

TEST
witness
attest, testament, detest, protestation

THE
god
atheist, theology, apotheosis, theocracy

THERM
heat
thermal, thermonuclear, hypothermia

TIM
fear, frightened
timid, intimidate, timorous

TOP
place
topic, topography, utopia

TORT
twist
distort, extort, tortuous

TORP
stiff, numb
torpedo, torpid, torpor

TOX
poison
toxic, intoxication

TRACT
draw
tractor, intractable, protract

TRANS
across, over, through, beyond
transgress, transient, transitory, translucent

TREM, TREP
shake
tremble, tremor, tremulous, trepidation, intrepid

TURB
shake
disturb, turbulent, perturbation

UMBR
shadow
umbrage, adumbrate, penumbra

UNI, UN
one
unify, unilateral, unanimous

URB
city
urban, urbane

VAC
empty
vacant, evacuate, vacuous

VAL, VAIL
value, strength
valid, valor, ambivalent, avail, prevail

VEN, VENT
come
convene, contravene, intervene, venue, circumvent, advent

VER
true
verity, verisimilitude, veracious, aver, verdict

VERB
word
verbose, verbiage, verbatim

VERT, VERS
turn
avert, revert, incontrovertible, divert, versatile, aversion

VICT, VINC
conquer
conviction, evict, evince, invincible

VID, VIS
see
evident, visage, supervise

VIL
base, mean
vile, vilify, revile

VIV, VIT
life
vivid, vital, convivial, vivacious

VOC, VOK, VOW
call, voice
equivocate, vociferous, evoke, invoke, avow

VOL
wish
voluntary, malevolent, benevolent

VOLV, VOLUT
turn, roll
revolve, evolve, convoluted

VOR
eat
devour, carnivore, voracious

Need Help Preparing
for the New SAT?

We've got some recommended reading

Also Available

Looking for More Ways to Build Your Vocabulary?

Try Kaplan's classic approach.

Coming soon!

Dr. Jekyll and Mr. Hyde: A Kaplan SAT Score-Raising Classic
(May 2005)

The Scarlet Letter: A Kaplan SAT Score-Raising Classic
(August 2005)

KAPLAN

Test Prep and Admissions
Published by Simon & Schuster

Ask for Kaplan wherever books are sold.

Need Help Writing Your College Application Essays?

Get Expert Advice from a Trusted Source

Education Program
Newsweek.

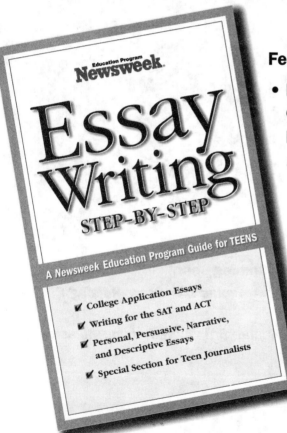

Features:

- **Details on the stages of the essay-writing process**

- **Sample essays**

- **In-depth advice for writing personal, persuasive, and narrative essays**

- **Writing for the SAT and ACT**

Test Prep and Admissions
Published by Simon & Schuster

Ask for Kaplan wherever books are sold.